We Wrestle Not:
A Kingdom Perspective of Spiritual Warfare

Christopher Turney

Unless otherwise indicated, all scripture quotations are taken from GOD'S WORD®, © 1995 God's Word to the Nations. Used by permission of Baker Publishing Group.
Scripture quotations marked "KJV", are from the *King James Version* of the Bible which is considered public domain within the United States of America.
Scripture quotations marked "LITV" are taken from the Literal Translation of the Holy Bible © 1976 – 2000 By Jay P. Green, Sr. Used by permission of the copyright holder.
Scripture quotations marked "TPT" are taken from The Passion Translation®, © 2017, 2018, 2020 by Passion & Fire Ministries, INC. Used by permission. All rights reserved
Scripture quotations marked (NLT) are taken from the Holy Bible, New Living Translation, copyright © 1996, 2004, 2015 by Tyndale House Foundation. Used by permission of Tyndale House Publishers, Inc., Carol Stream, Illinois 60188. All rights reserved.

Copyright © 2025 by Christopher Turney
Author and Publisher

All rights reserved. No part of this publication may be reproduced, stored in a retrieval system, or transmitted in any form or by any means, electronic, mechanical, photocopying, recording, or otherwise, without the prior written permission of the author, except for brief quotations used in reviews, teaching, or scholarly works.

ISBN: 979-8-218-80092-5

Dedication

Dedicated to those weary of the fight, and longing for the rest of the Lord. May you find comfort for your souls, and strength for your spirit. May His peace flood your heart, and may you discover His finished work.

Hebrews 4

Acknowledgements

I would like to acknowledge the Victorious One, Jesus, who made an open show of the devil through the blood of His cross.

A special thanks to the most beautiful and most God loving woman I know, my wife Jill. Without you by my side I couldn't live in my purpose. I love you!

To my beloved Bishop Gary Clowers, and the Pastor of my heart, Pastor Lydia. You both have stood by me through every trial and triumph, your support and undying love is so appreciated.

To my Kingdom Reign family, Treasure Coast and Ft. Wayne, you're the best! I love you and live to see you all find your finish! To all my friends laboring in ministry, I admire and love you all!

Contents

Introduction 1

Chapter One
    The Creator 5

Chapter Two
    The Bride 15

Chapter Three
    The Talking Serpent 25

Chapter Four
    The Roaring Lion 43

Chapter Five
    The Strategy And The Armor 67

Chapter Six
    The History Of Spiritual Warfare 81

Chapter Seven
    The Devil's Spotlight 127

Chapter Eight
    The Curse Stops Here 147

Chapter Nine
    Strategic-Level Warfare 155

Chapter Ten
    Identifying The Thief 169

Chapter Eleven
    An Open Invitation 193

Chapter Twelve
    Binding And Loosing 205

Chapter Thirteen
    Prophetic Strategies 215

Final Chapter
    Authorized Sons 221

INTRODUCTION

1983 was a life-changing year for me. In the spring of that year, I walked down the aisle of a Pentecostal church and surrendered to the Lord. That moment became a memorial, marking the beginning of a journey filled with trials and challenges that would ultimately shape the fabric of my spiritual life.

As my development in Christ continued, so did my hunger for Scripture. That hunger led me to devote several years of focused study at Christ for the Nations Bible Institute in Dallas, Texas. It was there that I was exposed to spiritual warfare. Though I had been introduced to the concepts of demonic activity and deliverance in my home church, it was during Bible school that the doctrine of spiritual warfare became etched into my doctrinal lens.

At my home church, teachings on deliverance and demonic possession were normal. While there was a prevailing belief that Christians couldn't "have" a devil, the awareness of spiritual conflict was constant. At Christ for the Nations, I encountered the writings of Lester Sumrall, Bob Larson, Frank Hammond, Charles Spurgeon, and C. Peter Wagner. Their words, often filled with vivid encounters, spiritual clashes, and victorious declarations, further shaped my perspective on spiritual warfare.

From that point forward, this subject not only informed my thinking, but it began to direct my ministry approach. Over time, the idea of spiritual warfare became just as fundamental as salvation or grace in much of the Church. What was once a doctrine had become a movement,

We Wrestle not...

complete with its own language, methodologies, and widespread appeal.

Terms like intercessory prayer, prayer walking, strategic spiritual mapping, and warfare praise became part of a growing lexicon. Believers were no longer just followers of Christ, they were soldiers, commissioned to battle the forces of darkness on behalf of their families, cities, and nations.

This movement gave birth to a zealous community of warriors, well-meaning, sincere, and passionate. Their hearts longed to see breakthrough, overcome strongholds, and defeat the devil in every area of life. Armed with swords and shields (both literal and figurative), many believers entered daily battles, opposing spiritual forces using the strategies they had been taught.

Prominent ministries published books and teachings detailing how to tear down strongholds, bind strongmen, cast out devils, and storm the gates of hell. Conferences were held. Prayer teams were mobilized. Some believers even sought spiritual guidance through counselors, dream interpreters, and, tragically, even psychics, crossing into occultic realms in search of deeper revelation.

In general, spiritual warfare has been understood as the engagement of demonic forces through various expressions such as intercessory prayer, prophetic decrees, warfare praise, and deliverance ministry. The focus has been on dislodging dark powers in specific regions, families, or personal lives.

But while it is clear from Scripture that we face an adversary, this book offers a different perspective, one deeply rooted in the finished work of Christ and the theology of rest. I do not deny the existence of demonic activity, nor do I propose the

We Wrestle not...

devil is some mythological symbol. He is real. But he is mostly irrelevant, because he is already defeated.

This book is not just a theological exploration; it is an exposé. It challenges a widespread mindset that has, intentionally or not, empowered the belief that God has a rival, that the war is still ongoing, and that the victory is still in question.

God's desire is for His Bride to be triumphant and at rest, clothed not in fear but in righteousness, adorned not in weariness but in glory.

C.S. Lewis captures this tension well:

"There are two equal and opposite errors into which our race can fall about the devils. One is to disbelieve in their existence.
The other is to believe, and to feel an excessive and unhealthy interest in them. They themselves are equally pleased by both errors and hail a materialist or a magician with the same delight."
— *C.S. Lewis, The Screwtape Letters*

Both errors distort the truth. It is unwise to ignore the enemy's existence, as Peter warned:

"Be alert and of sober mind. Your enemy the devil prowls around like a roaring lion looking for someone to devour."
— **1 Peter 5:8, NIV**

Yet to become so fixated on the devil that our prayer lives become filled with binding, rebuking, and confronting spiritual powers, hoping to gain victory, is equally dangerous. Why? Because our victory has already been secured.

We Wrestle not...

"Having disarmed the powers and authorities, He made a public spectacle of them, triumphing over them by the cross." — **Colossians 2:15, NIV**

Christ didn't just redeem us at the cross, He disarmed our enemy. His victory was not future tense. It was finished.

Today, the Church stands tired and battle-worn, scarred by a war she was never meant to fight again. The trumpet has been blown so many times that we've forgotten what it's like to rest. But I believe her finest hour is still ahead. And before she can be glorified in the earth, she must rediscover the rest of the Lord.

This book is a call to that rest.

We wrestle not.

CHAPTER ONE
THE CREATOR

"In the beginning God created the heavens and the earth." — **Genesis 1:1**

According to the Cambridge University Institute of Astronomy:

"There are something like 300 billion stars in the Milky Way. If 10 percent of them have planets, there are around 30 billion planets in our galaxy alone, and over 100 billion galaxies in the observable universe. That makes for a total of something in the order of 10^{21} planets in the observable universe." **(Cambridge Institute of Astronomy)**

And yet, God created all of it by the word of His mouth.

"By faith we understand that the universe was created by the word of God, so that what is seen was not made out of things that are visible." — **Hebrews 11:3, ESV**

"By the word of the Lord the heavens were made, and by the breath of His mouth all their host." — **Psalm 33:6, ESV**

Our God is an awesome God. He speaks, and galaxies burst forth. He exhales, and stars ignite.

Before time began, before man was formed, before rebellion ever arose, there was only God, and His voice. The universe did not emerge from chaos; it unfolded from command. The heavens did not evolve, they responded. His Word is not reactive, it is causative.

We Wrestle not...

He rules supreme as King, and His word is eternally established as both law and truth. Creation is not the result of divine labor; it is the manifestation of divine proclamation.

God's omnipotence is paradoxical to the human mind. Men display power through effort, through sweat, through striving. But God displays power through ease, through speech. He does not lift a finger; He simply opens His mouth. The entire cosmos came forth not through struggle, but through speech.

This is not poetic exaggeration; it is theological foundation. Speech, in the Kingdom, is not for communication alone; it is the vehicle of creation. In the beginning, there was no warfare, there was only Wordfare. The battleground of the Kingdom has always centered around voice, word, and agreement.

This is critical to understand, especially when considering one of the earliest events in the spiritual narrative: the fall of Lucifer.

"Now war arose in heaven, Michael and his angels fighting against the dragon. And the dragon and his angels fought back, but he was defeated, and there was no longer any place for them in heaven. And the great dragon was thrown down, that ancient serpent, who is called the devil and Satan, the deceiver of the whole world—he was thrown down to the earth, and his angels were thrown down with him." — **Revelation 12:7–9, ESV**

There's something deeply revealing in this passage: God never entered the fight. He did not personally contend with Satan. Instead, He delegated the battle to His angels, Michael and his host. The war in heaven was not a battle of rivals.

We Wrestle not...

The dragon, though described as "great," was defeated by angelic beings God Himself had created. His removal from heaven came at the hand of Michael, not at the hand of the Highest. The one who created the universe:

"By the word of the Lord the heavens were made, and by the breath of His mouth all their host." **Psalm 33:6 (ESV)**

God never felt threatened. He never descended to contend. Heaven was not destabilized. His throne was not shaken. Instead, the rebellion was crushed by those under His command. This shows that the enemy was never a true threat to God's supremacy, but rather a test of the created order's alignment with divine authority.

The God who breathed out planets didn't need to act directly. A command from His throne was enough to bring Lucifer's rebellion to an end. And once defeated, the enemy was cast out, not into a prison, not into a void, but to earth. He was cast out to earth, a mathematical phenomenon.

Based on observational data from NASA's Kepler and Hubble missions, as well as peer-reviewed studies (**e.g., Conselice et al., ApJ, 2016**), it is currently estimated that our Milky Way galaxy alone contains 160–640 billion planets. When extrapolated across the estimated 2 trillion galaxies in the observable universe, this results in approximately 200 sextillion planets.

If we conservatively use 100 billion stars per galaxy and 1 planet per star, that gives:

100 billion stars/galaxy × 2 trillion galaxies = 2×10^{23} planets (That's 200,000,000,000,000,000,000,000 planets 200 sextillions.)

Let that settle in.

We Wrestle not…

Of all the planets, sextillions in the observable universe, the destination for the defeated one was this planet. The very same one that God had already set aside to form man. This was no accident. This was not cosmic coincidence. This was divine strategy.

The choice of Earth as Satan's place of exile was not an afterthought, it was a masterstroke. While it may appear to the natural mind as a risk to place a deceiver on the same soil as His creation, God was revealing a pattern: the backdrop of rebellion becomes the birthplace of redemption. What Satan occupied temporarily, man was destined to inherit eternally.

"In Him we have obtained an inheritance, having been predestined according to the purpose of Him who works all things according to the counsel of His will." — **Ephesians 1:11, ESV**

God does all things with purpose. He consulted no one. He needed no counsel.

He was alone in His decision, and He chose to cast the enemy to the very place where He would soon place His image-bearers.

God was not concerned about man's co-existence with Satan on earth it was part of the plan.

The devil was not planted to defeat man, but to expose man's need for the Word. His presence would not diminish man's authority but reveal it. Where the serpent slithered, the son was meant to stand.

And then, in Genesis 1:26, we see something astounding:

We Wrestle not...

"Then God said, 'Let us make man in our image, after our likeness. And let them have dominion… over all the earth and over every creeping thing that creeps on the earth.'" — **Genesis 1:26, ESV**

God created man after Satan had already been cast down. And not only that, but He also gave man dominion over the very territory where Satan now resided.

Before Adam ever faced a temptation, he had already been given authority over the tempter

That's not just positional truth, it's prophetic intention. The man was not merely created in God's image, he was placed where rebellion once rose, to demonstrate divine order. Adam didn't need to rise in warfare; he needed only to remain in alignment. The authority was his by birth, not by battle.

This is not just poetic; it's prophetic. God placed man in authority over the very realm the enemy was exiled to. It was as if God was saying, "I don't need to fight you, I'll let My sons rule where you were cast."

Creation itself is a witness, not just to God's creative power, but to His unmatched sovereignty and strategic brilliance. The devil was not an obstacle to God's plan; he was a backdrop for it. And mankind, made in God's image, was set in place not to fight for dominion, but to walk in it.

Because the Creator does not just create things, He creates roles, realms, and rulership. He created man with a specific blueprint: "in Our image, after Our likeness." That phrase was not about anatomy, but about authority. The One who created galaxies now creates a governor on earth, a son-king to manifest His dominion in visible form.

We Wrestle not...

This is what distinguishes God as Creator. He doesn't just manufacture material, He instills meaning. Every act of creation was not just an exercise of power, but a revelation of purpose. The sun was to rule the day. The moon, to rule the night.

The stars, for signs and seasons. And man; man was created to rule on God's behalf.

"The heaven, even the heavens, are the Lord's; But the earth He has given to the children of men." — **Psalm 115:16, KJV**

God gave man the earth, not as a playground, but as a platform of partnership. The Creator, who had no need for assistance, chose to delegate His authority through image-bearing sons. It is one thing to make a universe; it is another to entrust it.

And yet, that is exactly what God did.

The Creator's brilliance is not just in the size of what He makes, but in the structure He sets. He creates order. He creates dominion. He creates government. Eden was not a botanical garden, it was a political territory. It was the original embassy of Heaven. It was where God's throne touched earth through the rule of His son.

That's why the temptation in Eden was not about fruit, it was about authority. The serpent's goal was not to introduce evil, it was to introduce doubt. To question the Word of the Creator is to challenge His order.

"Has God indeed said...?" — **Genesis 3:1**

The Creator, whose voice formed the cosmos, now has His Word questioned by a creature. But rather than reinforce the

We Wrestle not...

Word, man entertains the suggestion. And in that moment of disobedience, Adam does not lose a fight, he forfeits a trust.

The man's dominion, image, and voice was not stripped away by force, but surrendered through agreement. And yet, even this failure was foreseen by the One who creates not only beginnings but ends from the beginning.

"Known to God from eternity are all His works." — **Acts 15:18, NKJV**

That's what makes Him the Creator, not just in Genesis, but of the Lamb slain from the foundation of the world (Revelation 13:8). Before Adam breathed, the blood had already been determined. Before Eden was planted, the Cross had already been purposed. The Creator does not react. He pre-acts. He builds the solution before the problem emerges.

The devil has never caught Him by surprise.

So when we come to Revelation 5 and the scroll in the hand of Him who sits on the throne, we are not looking at the beginning of a rescue mission. We are witnessing the unfolding of what the Creator already established.

"Then I saw in the right hand of Him who was seated on the throne a scroll written within and on the back, sealed with seven seals." — **Revelation 5:1, ESV**

The scroll is written inside and out, just like the legal title deeds of ancient Israel (see Jeremiah 32). It represents authority. Inheritance. Ownership. It is the official document of rulership, what Adam forfeited, and what only one could reclaim: the Redeemer who was also the Creator.

We Wrestle not…

"Worthy are You to take the scroll and to open its seals, for You were slain, and by Your blood You ransomed people for God from every tribe and language and people and nation, and You have made them a kingdom and priests to our God, and they shall reign on the earth." — **Revelation 5:9–10, ESV**

Only the Creator can reclaim what was created. Only the One who made man could remake him. Only the One who formed Eden could restore it. Only the One who breathed out stars could breathe life back into dead sons.

The scroll is not just about judgment, it is about restoration. It is the moment the Creator, through the Lamb, reclaims the title deed of earth and reinstates sons to their original dominion.

And this is what undergirds all Kingdom understanding of spiritual warfare: The Creator is still seated. His throne has not moved. His Word has not failed. And His sons were not born to fight for victory, they were born from it.

We Wrestle not…

Reflection & Renewal:

1. What does it mean to you that God created everything by His Word, not His hands?
   How does this shape your understanding of power, effort, and spiritual authority?

2. Why is it significant that God never fought Lucifer personally but delegated the battle to angels?
   What does this reveal about the nature of Kingdom authority and divine strategy?

3. Out of 200 sextillion planets, why do you think God allowed Satan to be cast to earth, the same place He planned to create mankind?
   What does this say about God's confidence in the image He placed in man?

4. How does knowing Adam was given dominion before the serpent ever tempted him change your view of spiritual warfare?
   Are you living from a place of dominion or trying to earn it?

5. What authority or responsibility has God entrusted to you that may be currently challenged by deception instead of defeat?
   Reflect on how agreement with God's Word restores and activates dominion.

6. The Creator not only forms the universe, but also authors your purpose and calling.
   In what areas of your life do you need to return to His original blueprint rather than react to your environment?

We Wrestle not...

7. How does Revelation 5 connect back to Genesis 1? What does the scroll in Revelation represent considering mankind's original dominion?

8. Are you operating from the posture of a redeemed son, or from the mindset of a spiritual orphan still trying to fight for what Christ already secured?

9. What voices in your life mirror the serpent's question, "Has God said?"
   How will you confront and silence them with truth?

10. How does seeing God as Creator of both galaxies and government influence how you walk in Kingdom authority today?

CHAPTER TWO
THE BRIDE

Imagine receiving an invitation to attend the royal wedding in London. When you arrive, you smell the fragrance of beautiful and freshly cut flowers. Everything is extravagant, and no expense was spared for this glorious occasion.

Looking around this royal event, it is evident, that every guest, is donning their best choice of garment, and as you enter the cathedral, you hear glorious singing. Walking further into the beautifully decorated and majestic cathedral, an usher walks you to your seat.

Shortly after you are seated you see the groom, in all his excellence making his way to the altar, where he will stand expectantly awaiting his glorious bride.

The music crescendos to the bridal march.

The doors open and there sauntering down the aisle is a bride, clothed in a frayed and bloody garment, she is weak and unable to stand with her groom to be made one. It becomes clear to those witnessing this glorious event that something is terribly wrong, this is not the way it is supposed to be.

Some in attendance would be eagerly waiting for the punch line of this crudely played out prank. Many would maybe conclude that this isn't the bride at all, after all, what bride, at her most anticipated moment in life would present herself to her groom in this manner?

We Wrestle not...

To the surprise of many, the groom takes the hand of his bride and asks her gently,

"What happened to you, why is your garment tattered, and why are you wounded and bleeding?"

She responds with a weary but determined voice: *"I have been fighting in the battle".*

The groom replies, *"what battle?"*

Quickly she responds as though he should know the answer to his own question:

"You know, the battle against the enemy that wanted to steal, and kill and destroy me and keep me from this moment right here, right now when I would enter into an eternal place with you".

With great restraint but with obvious, perplexity the groom responds:

"Don't you remember, I took care of him so you wouldn't have to. I never wanted you to fight that battle, so I went and destroyed all his works, and I even made a spectacle of him in front of everyone.

This is our wedding day, I have been preparing for this day for a long time, and you were never to be presented to me like this.

I defeated all your enemies, all I wanted you to do was rest in what I had done, and to know, that I took care of everything. All I wanted you to do was to prepare yourself to see me today.

We Wrestle not…

You were supposed to make yourself ready for me, but you have come to me broken, beaten, and bloody, and now all these witnesses are wondering why I would not have provided for you better.

You have brought reproach to me, because you have come to me as a bride unkempt, and forsaken."

As the bride looks to her bridegroom for sympathy, he once again turns to her and says

"Do you not understand, the devil was never a threat to me, he was only a threat to you. I did not go into the earth and defeat him because he was a worthy opponent, I did that for you, because I love you!

You needed me to overthrow him, I had already proven my rule over him when I cast him as profane from my glorious kingdom. He wasn't threatening me or my power, he has never been a match for me."

I realize that this illustration is an extreme example of the actual event that awaits He and His church. But the time is now for the bride of our Lord to awake to the finished work of Calvary, and recognize His provisions are sufficient for our rest, and the that the victory won at the cross has made a way for us to bear His glory.

"And I John saw the holy city, new Jerusalem, coming down from God out of heaven, prepared as a bride adorned for her husband." — **Rev. 21:2 (KJV)**

His bride will be prepared and adorned! John continues in His Revelation of this bride called the Holy City.

"And there came unto me one of the seven angels which had the seven vials full of the seven last plagues, and talked with

We Wrestle not…

me, saying, Come hither, I will shew thee the bride, the Lamb's wife. And he carried me away in the spirit to a great and high mountain, and shewed me that great city, the holy Jerusalem, descending out of heaven from God, Having the glory of God: and her light was like unto a stone most precious, even like a jasper stone, clear as crystal; And had a wall great and high, and had twelve gates, and at the gates twelve angels, and names written thereon, which are the names of the twelve tribes of the children of Israel: On the east three gates; on the north three gates; on the south three gates; and on the west three gates. And the wall of the city had twelve foundations, and in them the names of the twelve apostles of the Lamb. And he that talked with me had a golden reed to measure the city, and the gates thereof, and the wall thereof. And the city lieth foursquare, and the length is as large as the breadth: and he measured the city with the reed, twelve thousand furlongs. The length and the breadth and the height of it are equal. And he measured the wall thereof, an hundred and forty and four cubits, according to the measure of a man, that is, of the angel.

And the building of the wall of it was of jasper: and the city was pure gold, like unto clear glass. And the foundations of the wall of the city were garnished with all manner of precious stones. The first foundation was jasper; the second, sapphire; the third, a chalcedony; the fourth, an emerald; The fifth, sardonyx; the sixth, sardius; the seventh, chrysolite; the eighth, beryl; the ninth, a topaz; the tenth, a chrysoprasus; the eleventh, a jacinth; the twelfth, an amethyst. And the twelve gates were twelve pearls; every several gate was of one pearl: and the street of the city was pure gold, as it were transparent glass. And I saw no temple therein: for the Lord God Almighty and the Lamb are the temple of it. And the city had no need of the sun, neither of the moon, to shine in it: for the glory of God did lighten it, and the Lamb is the light thereof.

We Wrestle not...

*And the nations of them which are saved shall walk in the light of it: and the kings of the earth do bring their glory and honour into it. And the gates of it shall not be shut at all by day: for there shall be no night there. And they shall bring the glory and honour of the nations into it. And there shall in no wise enter into it any thing that defileth, neither whatsoever worketh abomination, or maketh a lie: but they which are written in the Lamb's book of life." — **Rev. 21:9-27 (KJV)***

Now this description of the bride is vastly different than the one I illustrated. The details given by the Apostle John, reveal the depth of architectural thought and design.

This bride is the apple of His eye, the Church!

He is fully vested in her being all He created her to be. She belongs to Him, and her glory is His glory! This bride of Christ was born out of the devil's defeat at Calvary, and Her very existence is evidence of the triumph of the Bridegroom!

His death on the cross, dealt the crippling blow on Satan, for us the bride, not for Himself. At His last breath the victory bell sounded, when Jesus took His last breath, He released his Spirit. It was our victory through Christ!

The church was manifested after Jesus defeated the enemy on the cross. God never intended for us to fight devils, but rather to rule over them, and to command them, but not to war and wrestle with them. Jesus defeated our adversary before we the church, became the church, and before the bride was even born.

Amid tranquility Adams bride came on the scene, when God caused a deep sleep to fall upon Adam:

> *"And the Lord God caused a deep sleep to fall on Adam, and he slept; and He took one of his ribs, and closed up the flesh in its place. Then the rib which the Lord God had taken from man He made into a woman, and He brought her to the man."* — **Genesis 2:21–22 (NKJV)**

God put Adam into a deep sleep, prophetic of death. From Adam's opened side, God formed Eve, the first bride, from his own body, not from the dust.

THE FULFILLMENT IN CHRIST: THE LAST ADAM

> *"But when they came to Jesus and saw that He was already dead, they did not break His legs. But one of the soldiers pierced His side with a spear, and immediately blood and water came out."* — **John 19:33–34 (NKJV)**

Jesus, the Last Adam, was put into the deep sleep of death. His side was pierced under divine sovereignty. Blood and water flowed out, signifying the birth of the Church.

> *"And so it is written, 'The first man Adam became a living being.' The last Adam became a life-giving spirit."* — **1 Corinthians 15:45 (NKJV)**

BLOOD AND WATER: SYMBOLS OF REDEMPTION AND CLEANSING

> *"For the life of the flesh is in the blood..."* — **Leviticus 17:11 (NKJV)**

> *"...that He might sanctify and cleanse her with the washing of water by the word."* — **Ephesians 5:26 (NKJV)**

We Wrestle not...

"Unless one is born of water and the Spirit, he cannot enter the kingdom of God." — **John 3:5 (NKJV)**

"This is He who came by water and blood, Jesus Christ..." — **1 John 5:6 (NKJV)**

Blood = Atonement; Water = Cleansing and new birth. The Church is formed through the redemptive flow from Christ's side.

BONE OF HIS BONE: THE BRIDE SHARES HIS NATURE

"This is now bone of my bones and flesh of my flesh..." — **Genesis 2:23 (NKJV)**

"For we are members of His body, of His flesh and of His bones... This is a great mystery, but I speak concerning Christ and the church." — **Ephesians 5:30–32 (NKJV)**

The Church is Christ's Bride, bone of His bone, sharing His Spirit and life.

EVE FROM ADAM; THE CHURCH FROM CHRIST

"...that you may be married to another—to Him who was raised from the dead..." — **Romans 7:4 (NKJV)**

"Let us be glad and rejoice... for the marriage of the Lamb has come, and His wife has made herself ready." — **Revelation 19:7 (NKJV)**

Eve was not formed from dust, neither is the Church. The Church is birthed from the Last Adam's side, clothed in righteousness.

THE BRIDE IS BORN FROM A FINISHED WORK

"So when Jesus had received the sour wine, He said, 'It is finished!'" — **John 19:30 (NKJV)**

The Church is born from Christ's finished work. Adam was finished before Eve was formed. Christ completed redemption before the Church was revealed.

We Wrestle not…

Reflection & Renewal:

1. In what areas have I adopted a warfare mindset based on fear instead of covenant?
2. Do I believe that Jesus really finished the work, or am I still trying to earn or defend it?
3. How would my posture in prayer, worship, and life change if I truly lived as the Bride instead of a soldier?

CHAPTER THREE
THE TALKING SERPENT

In the Garden of Eden, God gave man dominion to rule and subdue the earth. This authority foreshadowed the dominion Christ, the Last Adam, would fully possess.

"And God said, Let us make man in our image, after our likeness: and let them have dominion over the fish of the sea, and over the fowl of the air, and over the cattle, and over all the earth, and over every creeping thing that creepeth upon the earth." — **Genesis 1:26 (KJV)**

Man's ability, or inability, to maintain this dominion would set the course for humanity. The first Adam was a living being who needed sustenance and structure. The Last Adam, Christ, gave life rather than just received it.

"The first man, Adam, became a living being. The last Adam became a life-giving spirit." — **1 Corinthians 15:45 (GW)**

Temptation is only powerful when it offers to fulfill a genuine need. The serpent identified a God-given design in humanity: the need not only for food, but for purpose and dominion. He offered Eve something that seemed to meet both.

"The woman saw that the tree had fruit that was good to eat, nice to look at, and desirable for making someone wise. So she took some of the fruit and ate it. She also gave some to her husband, who was with her, and he ate it." — **Genesis 3:6 (ERV)**

We Wrestle not...

The serpent was more cunning than any beast, and he twisted Eve's design against her to achieve his victory. She began surrendering her dominion the moment she entertained a conversation with a creature she had authority over. The serpent was not authorized to speak with God's delegated rulers.

Yet Eve engaged him, and through that conversation, her perception changed. Deception entered through dialogue. Dominion was compromised through conversation.

Adam and Eve were not just creations, they were God's authorized delegates on the earth. The dominion given to them covered all life, including the serpent. In a true Kingdom, one cannot address royalty without permission. Eve had dominion but entertained a voice beneath her rank.

"And God said, Let us make man in our image, after our likeness: and let them have dominion... over every creeping thing that creepeth upon the earth." — **Genesis 1:26 (KJV)**

Deception requires communication. The devil's weapon has always been words. Today, the talking serpent still operates through media, music, and messaging. He is powerless without communication.

Rebuking and shouting may feel powerful, but they may also be misplaced attempts to address what we've already been given dominion over.

"Death and life are in the power of the tongue..." — **Proverbs 18:21 (BBE)**

Sue Solis, a pastor's wife from Three Rivers, Michigan, once said:

"Words were not for conversation, but for creation."

We Wrestle not...

This is evident in the opening pages of Scripture. The very first activity of God is speech, not to chat, but to create. When God said, "Let there be light," there was no discussion, no debate, just immediate manifestation. In the Kingdom, words are not passive. They are active agents of reality.

This truth makes the conversation between Eve and the serpent more dangerous. It was not simply a dialogue; it was a distortion of design. As she spoke with the deceiver, she entered a creative moment, but not one aligned with her Creator. The enemy did not need power to overcome her; he simply needed access to her agreement. And once that was secured, a false reality was formed in her perception.

Adam and Eve lacked nothing in the garden. They were clothed in glory, surrounded by provision, and filled with purpose. But through the serpent's words, and Eve's willingness to entertain them, a perceived lack was created. "You will be like God," he said. But she was already made in His likeness. The lie did not introduce new information, it introduced discontentment through deception.

This is the creative danger of conversation with the adversary. When we entertain lies, we participate in crafting a false world, one where we are not enough, where God has withheld something, or where we must strive to become what we already are.

Words are for creation.

The question is: whose world are you building with yours?

Every agreement forms an atmosphere. Every conversation has consequences. Just as God's words formed the heavens, your words, fueled by either truth or deception, are forming the environment you live in.

This is why Paul urges us to "cast down imaginations" (2 Corinthians 10:5) and to be *"transformed by the renewing of our minds"* (Romans 12:2). Spiritual warfare begins with recognizing that our agreement determines atmosphere, and our words reveal whose reality we are reinforcing.

The Creator designed words to release order, life, and light. The enemy still attempts to twist that same creative mechanism to release confusion, death, and darkness. The question is never "Are we creating?" but "What are we creating, and with whom?"

> *"Faith convinces us that God created the world through his word. This means what can be seen was made by something that could not be seen."* — **Hebrews 11:3 (GW)**

Man, made in God's likeness, was given the power to speak and declare. Adam named the animals and identified Eve with his words. This same authority is echoed by Jesus:

> *"Behold, I give unto you power to tread on serpents and scorpions, and over all the power of the enemy: and nothing shall by any means hurt you."* — **Luke 10:19 (KJV)**

Even though Genesis and Luke were written generations apart, the serpent remained a symbol of the enemy. Jesus encountered demonic spirits and never held casual conversation with them, only authoritative commands. His only recorded dialogue was during His wilderness temptation, and even then, His responses were rooted in Scripture.

> *"And when the devil had ended all the temptation, he departed from him for a season."* — **Luke 4:13 (KJV)**

We Wrestle not...

Jesus mentioned the Kingdom of God 119 times in the Gospels. One such reference helps establish its priority:

"But seek ye first the kingdom of God, and his righteousness; and all these things shall be added unto you." — **Matthew 6:33 (KJV)**

The temptation of Jesus is mentioned in three of the four Gospels. It came immediately after His baptism, when heaven declared His identity.

"And Jesus, when he was baptized, went up straightway out of the water: and, lo, the heavens were opened unto him, and he saw the Spirit of God descending like a dove, and lighting upon him: And lo a voice from heaven, saying, This is my beloved Son, in whom I am well pleased." — **Matthew 3:16–17 (KJV)**

"And immediately the Spirit driveth him into the wilderness. And he was there in the wilderness forty days, tempted of Satan; and was with the wild beasts; and the angels ministered unto him." — **Mark 1:12–13 (KJV)**

"And when the tempter came to him, he said, If thou be the Son of God, command that these stones be made bread." — **Matthew 4:3 (KJV)**

The Spirit led Jesus into the wilderness to confirm what the Father had just said. The enemy's tactic was the same as in Eden: to challenge God's word and provoke doubt in identity.

Jesus didn't respond to Satan's voice, He responded to His Father's word.

"For we have not an high priest which cannot be touched with the feeling of our infirmities; but was in all points

tempted like as we are, yet without sin." — **Hebrews 4:15 (KJV)**

Scripture makes us aware of the enemy's deceptive nature. His first act in Eden was to twist God's words.

"Now the serpent was more subtil than any beast of the field which the LORD God had made. And he said unto the woman, Yea, hath God said, Ye shall not eat of every tree of the garden?" — **Genesis 3:1 (KJV)**

THE HELPER WAS THE SERPENT'S ASSIGNMENT

The serpent didn't confront the head, He deceived the help meet.

The serpent didn't speak to Adam. He spoke to Eve.

This was not just circumstantial, it was strategic.

Eve wasn't just another person in the garden. She was the helper, the Hebrew says the *ezer kenegdo*, the one taken from Adam's side, designed by God to assist, support, and multiply the man's assignment.

She was the answer to what God called "not good."

"It is not good that man should be alone; I will make him a helper comparable to him." **(Genesis 2:18, NKJV)**

We Wrestle not...

When things are NOT GOOD the answer is a help meet.

Adam's aloneness didn't require romance, it didn't require emotional security, it didn't necessitate a best friend, it required suitable support.

Eve was not the weaker one, she was the strategic one.

The multiplier.
The stabilizer.
And that's exactly why she was targeted.

The serpent bypassed the head and came for the help. Why?

Because the vision needs support.
- Ministry needs support.
- Marriages need support.
- Churches, families, and Kingdom assignments cannot function without suitable support.

And if the serpent can distract the support system, he can disrupt the whole order The talking serpent doesn't always come for the appointed leader, he talks to the ones holding it up.

The Local Church: Where the support makes the difference

Helpers uphold the atmosphere, the administration, and the anointing. They are the support. They are the compatible companions God has chosen to be the help meet for purpose.

Because if the helper is confused, discouraged, offended, or deceived, the entire structure starts to weaken.

We Wrestle not...

Whether it's:
- Children's ministry
- Cleaning and maintenance teams
- Youth leaders
- Media and sound crews
- Hospitality
- Financial partners and givers

These are not background roles. They are foundation roles. And because of that, they are often object of the subtle serpent, not through calamity, but through the whisperings of projected thoughts.

This is why we must be sober and vigilant, not just as leaders, but as helpers.

Whether you're an assistant, an intercessor, a spouse, a supporter of vision, or a worker in God's house, the serpent speaks to the help.

Ever wonder why, shortly after you commit to serve, commit your support, you began to feel dissuaded from it?

The moment someone commits to serve, the target is set, and the projections begin:
- "They don't appreciate me."
- "I'm the only one showing up."
- "I'm not really needed here."
- "I'm too tired to keep doing this."

But here's the trick: these thoughts don't sound like the serpent. They sound like you.

We Wrestle not…

THE WHISPER THAT SHAKES THE HOUSE

One of the most dangerous aspects of the serpent's subtlety is how he whispers in ways that sound like our own inner voice. He projects thoughts, doubts, and fears, but masks them as if they originated from within us.

"Now the serpent was more cunning than any beast of the field…" **(Genesis 3:1, NKJV)**

He doesn't roar. He whispers.
He doesn't accuse. He suggests.
He doesn't say, "You're unworthy." Instead, the thought forms: "I'm not worthy."
This is psychological warfare of the highest order.
He plants the thought, but lets you believe you grew it.

He doesn't need to possess you; he just needs to influence your inner dialogue.

He gets you to think it's your idea.
He lets you hear yourself say it internally, and the soul starts watering the seed.

The war is in the thought realm.

And many of God's people are losing battles not because they sinned, but because they believed.

They believed something that wasn't true.

We must ask ourselves: *'Is this thought in alignment with God's Word, or is this a projection from the serpent?'*

Because every thought has a source, either from the Spirit of Truth or from the father of lies. Don't let the enemy pitch a tent in your mind and call it your personality.

We Wrestle not...

Don't wear the serpent's suggestion like an identity.

Just because it sounds like you doesn't mean it is you.

Let the mind of Christ be in you and silence the subtle voice that doesn't belong. He doesn't come with a command. He doesn't even come with a suggestion that sounds foreign. Instead, he crafts thoughts to sound like they originated from within you.

Instead of saying, *'You shouldn't do that,'* he plants the thought, *'I shouldn't do that.'*

He subtly shifts the voice so that it feels personal.

Now it's not the enemy's voice you're hearing, it feels like your own conscience. This is psychological warfare of the highest order. He makes the lie feel like it's been living inside you all along. And once you take ownership of the thought, you begin to live it out.

Why? Because it plays upon our inherent need and desire to be in control of our own lives.

He knows that if you believe it's your own idea, it's acceptable.

Ever had anyone tell you concerning another person, *"just let them think it was their idea and they will do it"* or *"If it's not their idea they won't want to do it, you have to let them think it was their idea"*

But we must be discerning. Every thought must be tested. Every internal whisper must be measured against the voice of the Word. If it does not align with truth, then it is not from the Spirit of God, even if it sounds like it came from you.

We Wrestle not...

So the helper who was once joyful in their service becomes:
- Quietly bitter
- Quietly withdrawn
- Quietly offended
- Quietly burdened

And all of it began, not with a sin, but with thought.

THE BATTLE IS IN THE MIND, NOT THE SPIRIT

"Casting down arguments and every high thing that exalts itself against the knowledge of God, bringing every thought into captivity to the obedience of Christ." — **2 Corinthians 10:5, (NKJV)**

Many of God's people are losing spiritual momentum, not because they disobeyed, but because they believed something that wasn't true.

If the serpent can cause the help to hesitate, the house starts to shake.
If he can confuse the helper, he can clog the pipeline of ministry.
If he can plant a lie in the loyal, he can derail the vision without touching the leader.

Discernment Is the Weapon

We must ask ourselves:

"Is this thought from God, or is this a projection from the serpent?"

Because every thought has a source:
- The Spirit of Truth
- Or the father of lies

We Wrestle not...

Just because it sounds like you, doesn't mean it came from you.

Don't let your feelings become your filters.

The mind of Christ is your safeguard. And discernment is the defense of every helper.

Final Word: Helpers Need to be Covered

Whether you vacuum the floors, preach the Word, or sow in secret, helpers are need covering.

The serpent still whispers.
But now we recognize the voice.
Now we take thoughts captive.
Now we stand with discernment and declare:

Declaration:

The helpers are covered!
The helpers are guarded by grace!
The helpers are full of discernment!
And the days of help being deceived are over!
We no longer confuse our thoughts with his projections.

The mind of Christ is our weapon, and we will not be moved by the talking serpent.

Satan's cunning opened the door for sin and death. He was cast to earth, scheming to gain advantage over man. Paul writes about the need to recognize these tactics:

We Wrestle not...

"To whom ye forgive any thing, I forgive also... Lest Satan should get an advantage of us: for we are not ignorant of his devices." — **2 Corinthians 2:10–11 (KJV)**

Paul states that being aware of his devices is a key to maintaining an upper hand with our adversary. This truth has been one of many building blocks, in the establishment of modern-day warfare doctrine.

For many in the church, the enemy became somewhat of an object of study. Because life is constant with struggle and tribulation, the devil was the prime suspect, and therefore was the focus of Christian "investigation". Like committed detectives, believers throughout history have dedicated their lives to catching the devil and sentencing him to an eternal punishment in the abyss.

This investigation has caused many to map out cities and determine the strongman's grip on the region. It has been the basis for all night praise and prayer gatherings, to dismantle and disengage demonic activity. Banners have been made, spiritual swords have been drawn, songs have been sung, declarations and decrees have been shouted from church sanctuaries around the globe, and we have plead the blood from midnight to morning.

Books have captured these practices and have been published worldwide as instruction manuals on how to storm the gates of hell to take back what has been stolen and to loose the bands of wickedness off of our loved ones.

Yet the original battleground was and still is conversation. Dominion is lost or won at the level of thought and voice. Silence the talking serpent in your life, by only holding conversation with the Creator!

We Wrestle not...

The adversary's strength is not in force, but in feedback. He does not have omniscience. He does not read minds. He must rely on conversation, on words spoken, to discern which thoughts landed and what ideas have taken root. He sends projections like flaming darts, but he only knows they've struck when we respond, either with our mouths or our minds.

Imagine sending a text message: until it's answered, there is no confirmation that it was received. The devil's projections operate the same way. The "read receipt" comes when we engage. When we speak back. When we muse aloud. When we confess doubt. Without conversation, he has no confirmation.

This is why idle words are so dangerous and why Jesus warned that every careless word will be judged (Matthew 12:36). Words are not meaningless, they are measurements. They mark spiritual agreements and expose mental environments. They do not fall to the ground; they form the ground you walk on.

"Death and life are in the power of the tongue..." — **Proverbs 18:21**

What we say informs more than people, it informs principalities. When we voice frustration, fear, unbelief, or complaint, we may be unintentionally educating our adversary, giving him insight he wouldn't have known apart from our own declarations.

The serpent's strategy hasn't changed: provoke conversation, gather intel, then press further. But here's the truth: silence can be a strategy. Refusing to respond, staying rooted in God's Word, and declining to debate darkness is not weakness, it is wisdom.

We Wrestle not…

Even Jesus, when tempted in the wilderness, did not speak to the devil, He spoke from the Father.

Every word He released was not a reaction to Satan's provocation but a revelation of the Father's voice.

"Man shall not live by bread alone, but by every word that proceeds from the mouth of God." — **Matthew 4:4, NKJV**

This was not just Scripture quoting; it was Sonship expressed. Jesus wasn't engaging in spiritual sparring; He was echoing His Father. His responses were not crafted to combat the devil but to remain in covenant. He answered nothing that wasn't already authored in heaven.

This reveals a powerful Kingdom principle:

The safest way to respond to the adversary is to not respond to him at all, but to respond to God.

Every time the enemy speaks, the question is not, "What do I say back?" but "What is the Father saying?"

This is the secret of spiritual authority: alignment, not argument. Sons do not negotiate with serpents; they agree with their Source. The moment we leave that posture, we risk doing what Eve did: entertaining what should have been cast down.

This is the maturity God is calling His sons into: not just the ability to speak, but the wisdom to discern when and what to say. The tongue is not a toy it is a tool. It either collaborates with Heaven or gives clues to hell.

We Wrestle not...

We must remember; in the Kingdom, words are always building something. The question is never, "Am I creating?" but rather, "What am I creating, and who am I creating it with?"

We Wrestle not...

Reflection & Renewal:

1. What does the Creator's use of words to form the universe reveal about the power of your own words? Are your words creating peace, order, and faith, or fear, confusion, and doubt?

2. What was Satan's goal in speaking with Eve, and how does that compare to how he attempts to speak with you?
   Have you unknowingly co-authored confusion by engaging in internal dialogue with lies?

3. When God cast Satan to earth, He knew He would also create man from that same ground.
   What does this say about God's trust in what He placed inside of you?

4. Jesus never answered the devil on His own, He echoed the voice of His Father.
   In moments of temptation or pressure, are your responses reactive, or are they rooted in divine relationship?

5. How often do you give the adversary information by what you say aloud?
   Consider the weight of your words and whether they are equipping Heaven, or exposing you to unnecessary warfare.

6. Satan's strategy begins with suggestion.
   Have you mistaken demonic projections for personal thoughts? How can you better discern what is from God and what is not?

CHAPTER FOUR
THE ROARING LION

"Be sober, be vigilant; because your adversary the devil walks about like a roaring lion, seeking whom he may devour." — **1 Peter 5:8, KJV**

There is no prevailing argument among believers concerning the existence of the devil or his destructive intent. Scripture makes it clear, he's relentlessly hunting, roaring with intimidation, seeking those he may consume. But Peter's warning is not a declaration of war, it's a call to sobriety. The danger is not the lion's claws. It's the believer's "drunkenness".

To be sober means to live without the dulling influence of deception. To forsake mixture, a Babylonian way of thinking. It is to see clearly. Nahum paints a similar picture:

"While they are entangled as thorns, and while they are drunk as drunkards, they shall be devoured like stubble fully dry." — **Nahum 1:10, KJV**

Doctrinal drunkenness and intoxication, renders a person vulnerable to deception, pride, idolatry, and religious mixture. Peter's warning is not about demons storming the gates; it's about believers stumbling in the dark because they've lost clarity.

Lions hunt at night, not because they see better, but because their prey sees worse.

We Wrestle not...

"Let us not sleep, as others do, but let us watch and be sober. For those who sleep, sleep at night, and those who get drunk are drunk at night." — **1 Thessalonians 5:6–7, NKJV**

The roaring lion uses darkness as his advantage. But the true threat to believers isn't the roar, it's the intoxication. And Scripture reveals what that intoxication looks like.

"With whom the kings of the earth committed fornication, and the inhabitants of the earth were made drunk with the wine of her fornication." — **Revelation 17:2, KJV**

The great harlot of Babylon has made the world drunk, not just with pleasure, but with confusion by mixture. The name Babylon literally means confusion by mixture. Thus, Babylonian religion is idolatry cloaked in spirituality. It is doctrine mixed with deception. Like a cocktail, it numbs the conscience while claiming to offer comfort.

Many in the Church are not drunk on outright heresy, but on "mixed drinks", sermons that blend truth with legalism, freedom with fear, grace with performance. It feels spiritual, but it clouds the mind.

What belongs in a covenant, the harlot sells, without promise, without trust, and only for profit.

Likewise, religion offers a form of godliness without transformation. It's a transaction, not a relationship. It requires performance but offers no peace. It becomes idolatry, pleasure without purity, power without surrender.

"Rebellion is as the sin of witchcraft, and stubbornness is as iniquity and idolatry." — **1 Samuel 15:23, KJV**

Idolatry begins with a refusal to obey. It is the insistence on doing things our way while still invoking God's name. And

We Wrestle not...

this is what makes mixture so dangerous, it masquerades as devotion.

Jesus confronted this in Laodicea:

"Because you are lukewarm, and neither cold nor hot, I will vomit you out of My mouth." — **Revelation 3:16, NKJV**

Lukewarm is the product of mixture. And mixture disorients the believer until they can no longer discern the lion's roar from the Spirit's voice.

When Israel was taken into Babylonian captivity, they were stripped of their language, their names were changed, and their diets were altered. Babylon doesn't just aim to imprison the body, it aims to confuse the soul.

The Theology of Mixture: God Hates the Blend

In Deuteronomy 22:9–11, God gives symbolic instructions:

"You shall not sow your vineyard with different kinds of seed, lest the yield of the seed which you have sown and the fruit of your vineyard be defiled."

"You shall not plow with an ox and a donkey together."

"You shall not wear a garment of different sorts, such as wool and linen mixed together."

These laws weren't merely agricultural or fashion advice, they were prophetic pictures of purity. Let's unpack each:

We Wrestle not...

Mixed Seeds – Hybrid Identity and Confusion

Sowing two kinds of seed into the same soil is a metaphor for spiritual mixture. The resulting hybrid crop doesn't reproduce properly and often lacks the integrity of either original seed.

Mixing seed represents the blending of God's Word with other philosophies, doctrines, or cultures.

"A little leaven leavens the whole lump." — **Galatians 5:9**

This produces confusion in the people. It dilutes the purity of God's Word and compromises harvest integrity.

Mixed Seed: The Confusion of Identity

"You shall not sow your vineyard with different kinds of seed, lest the yield... be defiled." — **Deuteronomy 22:9**

In Scripture, seed represents the Word (Luke 8:11). When God forbids sowing two kinds of seed into the same field, He is illustrating a principle: two conflicting words planted in the same soil will produce confusion, not clarity.

This is precisely what has happened in much of modern Christianity. The soil of the heart is often sown with mixed doctrine, the Word of God mingled with the traditions of men, truth laced with contradiction. One of the most dangerous mixtures is the blend of "sinner" identity with saint reality.

We hear phrases like:

"I'm just a sinner saved by grace..."

We Wrestle not...

But this is a hybrid identity, a mixture of who you were and who you are. It sounds humble, but it's theologically toxic. The believer is not both sinner and saint. You were a sinner. You were dead in trespasses and sins. But now:

"If anyone is in Christ, he is a new creation; old things have passed away; behold, all things have become new." — **2 Corinthians 5:17, NKJV**

"He made Him who knew no sin to be sin for us, that we might become the righteousness of God in Him." — **2 Corinthians 5:21, NKJV**

You are not two people. You are not half-redeemed, half-broken. You are not a sinner and a saint.

That is Babylonian theology, confusion by mixture. The source of intoxication. This makes us vulnerable to the roaring lion.

Babylon means "confusion by mixing."
God never called His sons to live with a split identity.

When the Church sows this kind of seed, it raises up double-minded believers, people who feel forgiven one day and condemned the next, saved but unworthy, redeemed but still enslaved to an old name.

"A double-minded man is unstable in all his ways." — **James 1:8 (NKJV)**

This mixture intoxicates the Church. It produces an identity crisis, not transformation. A believer who believes he is still a sinner will live under sin-consciousness, always striving, never resting, never reigning.

Mixed seed creates mixed fruit.

It doesn't multiply, it confuses.
It doesn't nourish, it poisons.
It doesn't free, it binds with religious humility that God never authored.

But the pure seed of the Kingdom declares:

"You are a chosen generation, a royal priesthood, a holy nation, His own special people..." — **1 Peter 2:9 (NKJV)**

This is the power of unmixed seed, clarity of identity, boldness in sonship, and fruit that reflects the DNA of Heaven.

Unequally Yoked, Imbalanced Labor and Direction

Plowing with an ox and a donkey yoked together reflects unequal partnership. The ox is clean, strong, obedient. The donkey is unclean, stubborn, and incompatible.

This speaks to covenants or partnerships that cannot produce fruit, because they do not walk in the same nature or rhythm. It is a picture of ministry alliances, marriages, or spiritual labor unequally aligned. The result is not just inefficiency, but distortion of Kingdom purpose.

"Do not be unequally yoked together with unbelievers..." — **2 Corinthians 6:14 (NKJV)**

Being unequally yoked is not merely about contrasting belief systems; it's about conflicting wills, natures, and objectives. It's about attempting to walk in step with someone, or something, that does not share the same rhythm, burden, or vision.

We Wrestle not...

The ox is steady, enduring, and submitted to the plow. It moves forward even when the soil is resistant.

The donkey, by contrast, is stubborn, unyielding, and unpredictable. It may start with enthusiasm but resist when the path becomes narrow, or the burden becomes weighty.

To yoke an ox with a donkey is to bind two creatures with different instincts and expectations, creating constant tension in the field.

The ox wants to finish. The donkey wants to quit before the work is complete. The ox yields to the master. The donkey often resists even a gentle pull.

This isn't just about marriage or friendship, it's about partnerships, ministry alliances, and any assignment requiring shared labor.

Agreement is not sameness, it is alignment.

"Can two walk together, unless they are agreed?" — **Amos 3:3 (NKJV)**

Being unequally yoked is not just about where we stand, it's about where we're going, and how we plan to get there.

To be unequally yoked is to frustrate the field, hinder progress, and distort the rows of harvest. You may both be tied to the same plow, but if one is pulling and the other is resisting, the furrows will be crooked, and the fruit will be delayed.

In the Kingdom, agreement is not optional, it's essential. Agreement is not passive, it is intentional unity of purpose, timing, and submission to the same voice.

We Wrestle not...

This is why God hates mixture. Not because of personal preferences, but because mixture brings misalignment, and misalignment compromises movement.

Mixed Garments – Confused Identity

In ancient times, garments signified identity, class, priesthood, and purpose.
- Priests wore holy garments.
- Nobles wore linen.
- Prophets wore mantles.

Mixed fabrics represent a tearing of identity, trying to be two things at once.
- Wool (from sheep) represents the flesh, it's hot, heavy, irritating.
- Linen represents righteousness, cool, pure, light.

"Fine linen is the righteous acts of the saints." — **Revelation 19:8 (NKJV)**

To mix wool and linen is to mingle works and righteousness, flesh and spirit, or worldliness and holiness, and God rejects it.

Laodicea: The Mixture That Made God Vomit

"I know your works, that you are neither cold nor hot. I could wish you were cold or hot. So then, because you are lukewarm, and neither cold nor hot, I will vomit you out of My mouth." — **Revelation 3:15–16 (NKJV)**

Lukewarmness is not about temperature but mixture, a blend of two incompatible states. The Laodicean church was rich in worldly goods, but poor in spiritual substance. They blended prosperity with pride, religion with compromise, and worship with apathy.

This "vomiting" symbolizes divine rejection of mixture. God would rather deal with cold (outright rebellion) or hot (zeal) than the delusion of mixture.

Babylon: The Mother of Mixture

Babylon, in both the Old and New Testaments, represents systemic mixture. The name Babel means "confusion," and it originated with a rebellion against God (Genesis 11).

"Come, let Us go down and there confuse their language, so that they will not understand one another's speech." — **Genesis 11:7 (NKJV)**

Babel was humanity's attempt to blend heaven and earth on their own terms. They used human unity, bricks instead of stones (uniformity over uniqueness), and built a name for themselves.

In Revelation 17, Babylon is portrayed as a harlot, clothed in purple and scarlet, riding the beast, holding a golden cup of abominations.

"And on her forehead a name was written: MYSTERY, BABYLON THE GREAT, THE MOTHER OF HARLOTS AND OF THE ABOMINATIONS OF THE EARTH." — **Revelation 17:5 (NKJV)**

Why is she a harlot? Because she takes what belongs in covenant and offers it to all nations, without loyalty, without truth, without holiness.

We Wrestle not...

Mixture is her trade.
- Spiritual fornication is her method.
- Compromise for influence is her mission.
- Confusion through blend is her mark.

This spirit of Babylon creeps into the Church when we merge culture with Kingdom, truth with tolerance, and God's ways with man's wisdom.

This is not just a picture of moral compromise; it is a prophetic warning against spiritual ministry without covenantal relationship. She mirrors the very thing Jesus warned His Church against, mixture, ambition, and influence without intimacy.

Jesus didn't say, *"Go into all the world and get decisions."* He said, *"Go and make disciples of all nations."* — **Matthew 28:19 (NKJV)**

Discipleship requires covenant, time, investment, and relationship. Babylon's wine intoxicates leaders and ministries with a different gospel, one of conversion without commitment, mass appeal without spiritual formation, and global reach without Kingdom depth.

Converts can be counted. Disciples must be formed.
Converts fill rosters. Disciples carry crosses.
Converts may swell the crowd. Disciples advance the Kingdom.

Babylon's system celebrates influence without intimacy, platforms without process, and ministry to the nations without marriage to the King. This is the seduction of the harlot: to give the appearance of Kingdom expansion while abandoning the very nature of the King.

We Wrestle not...

"With her the kings of the earth committed fornication, and the inhabitants of the earth were made drunk with the wine of her fornication." — **Revelation 17:2 (NKJV)**

We often think this refers only to political leaders or world rulers. But from a Kingdom perspective, this passage is a direct warning to us, the sons of God, the kings and priests who are called to rule with Christ.

"And has made us kings and priests to our God; And we shall reign on the earth." — **Revelation 5:10, NKJV**

"To Him who loved us and washed us from our sins in His own blood, and has made us kings and priests..." — **Revelation 1:5–6, NKJV**

We are the kings of the earth, not because of earthly crowns, but because of heavenly calling. And Babylon's seduction is aimed precisely at us.

What does it mean that the kings of the earth committed fornication with her?

It means that those set apart to reign became entangled in compromise. Those given authority began using it for personal gain, public approval, or cultural assimilation. It is a betrayal of covenant for counterfeit influence.

Babylon doesn't chase rebels, she seduces rulers.

She offers a shortcut to impact, a platform without purity, a reach without relationship. She feeds the ego of kings who forget they are first sons. She seduces the called by offering influence without intimacy, ministry without holiness, revelation without repentance.

We Wrestle not…

One may ask how can those washed in His blood and redeemed, commit fornication with this harlot?

Revelation 18:4 gives a clear call to God's people:

*"Come out of her, **My people**, lest you share in her sins…"*
— **Revelation 18:4**

That means some of His people were in Babylon, drinking, compromising, mixing.

Revelation 1:6 is a position.
Revelation 17:2 is a perversion.

We were made kings. But the question is, will we reign as sons, or fornicate by intoxication?

The Wine of Her Fornication: Drunk Kings Forget Their Crown

The text says the inhabitants of the earth were "made drunk" with the wine of her fornication.

Drunkenness, in Scripture, always symbolizes a loss of discernment, clarity, and judgment. When kings drink from Babylon's cup:

- They forget their Father.
- They misrepresent their Kingdom.
- They exchange glory for gain.
- They sell their inheritance for applause.

Like Esau, they trade their birthright for a bowl of satisfaction.

We Wrestle not…

And this is why the lion roars, not to destroy authority, but to devour it when it's misused.
A drunken king is a vulnerable one.

The Call: Come Out From Her, My People

Again:

"Come out of her, <u>my people</u>, lest you share in her sins, and lest you receive of her plagues." — **Revelation 18:4, NKJV**

This is not a call to leave a city, it's a call to break agreement with a system.

If we are kings, then our purity matters. Our covenant matters. Our influence must be born in the bridal chamber, not in Babylon's bed.

The seduction is real, but so is the remedy:
Stay sober. Stay set apart. Stay seated with Christ.

This is the wine of compromise, where the Church becomes a vendor of sacred things without the vow of faithfulness. Ministry becomes a transaction, not a covenant. The Church becomes a performance stage, not a bridal chamber.

The harlot has a cup. The bride has a covenant.

The harlot seeks the nations for profit. The bride seeks the nations for the Lamb's reward.

So we must ask ourselves: Are we discipling sons, or collecting salvation decisions? Are we entering nations with a ring of covenant or a cup of compromise?

We Wrestle not…

Biblical Examples of Mixture and Its Consequences

Samaria (2 Kings 17:33)

They feared the Lord, yet served their own gods…"

This verse is one of the clearest examples of mixture in worship, spiritual intoxication. The people feared the Lord (outward reverence) but served other gods (divided loyalty). Their worship was syncretistic, an unholy blend of Yahweh reverence and pagan practice.

They didn't reject the Lord; they simply added to Him, and that's exactly what Babylonian mixture does: it preserves the appearance of God while perverting the purity of devotion.

This verse perfectly parallels the modern Church's struggle:
- Believers claim to fear the Lord, go to church, worship, read the Bible.
- But simultaneously serve the gods of culture, performance, mammon, platform, self-preservation.
- Their spiritual practice is "according to the rituals of the nations", they adopt the methods, mindset, and mixture of the world while still claiming covenant with God.

This is not rebellion by rejection, it is rebellion by mixture.

And like Israel, this leads to spiritual confusion, broken identity, and eventual judgment if not repented of.

A dual allegiance that resulted in generational compromise and idolatry.

We Wrestle not...

We Are Not Under Attack, We Are Under the Influence

When the chaos of our own choices begins to manifest, broken relationships, dried-up fruit, spiritual confusion, and exhaustion, we often say, *"The devil is attacking me."*

But the truth is far more sobering.

What we call an attack may really be the result of intoxication.
Not an assault from a roaring lion, but the side effects of drinking from Babylon's cup.
We're not wrestling, we're wavering.
We're not being devoured, we're being deceived.
The warfare isn't external, it's internal.
We are under the influence, not under attack.

This is the genius of Satan's modern strategy:

He has repackaged spiritual intoxication as spiritual warfare.

He has trained a generation of believers to attribute to him what is the fruit of their own mixture.

Again:

"They feared the Lord, yet served their own gods..." — **2 Kings 17:33**

We cry out, *"Lord, deliver us from the enemy!"*

But heaven is asking, *"Why are you still drinking with him?"*

We quote, *"When the enemy comes in like a flood..."*

We Wrestle not…

But often, the flood was not the enemy, it was our disobedience. The "enemy" is the consequence of divided loyalty and spiritual syncretism.

The roaring lion isn't pouncing, he's patiently watching, waiting for those too spiritually disoriented to remember who they are.

Babylon doesn't just deceive with idols; it intoxicates with doctrine. Warfare isn't what we're fighting off, it's what we're feeding on.

The Call to Sobriety

This isn't a call to war.
It's a call to sobriety.
To repent of mixture, to renounce Babylon's wine, and to return to the simplicity of Christ.

"Be sober, be vigilant…" — **1 Peter 5:8 (NKJV)**

If we are going to wrestle, let it not be against devils that have already been defeated, but against the drunkenness of our own confusion, the teachings that dishonor the finished work, and the identities that no longer fit us.

We don't need to fight harder, we need to think clearer.
We don't need louder prayers, we need a cleaner cup.

The solution is not more warfare, it is more clarity. More agreement. More alignment.

We Wrestle not...

Aaron's Golden Calf

He declared a feast "to the LORD," yet built a calf, a blend of Yahweh worship and Egyptian practice. God did not accept it. He judged it. (Exodus 32)

King Saul's Partial Obedience

He obeyed part of God's instruction but spared what he considered useful. His kingdom was torn from him, not for rebellion alone, but for mixture under the guise of obedience. (1 Samuel 15)

Ananias and Sapphira

They blended generosity with deception. They gave part while pretending it was whole. The result: judgment and death. (Acts 5)

God's Call to Purity and Distinction

God's command has always been:

"Be holy, for I am holy." — **1 Peter 1:16 (NKJV)**

Holiness is not perfection; it is separation unto God. It is refusal to mix light with darkness, truth with error, worship with flesh.

Jesus is returning for a bride without spot or wrinkle, not a hybrid, half-holy church entangled in Babylon's system. The Kingdom is a culture of clarity, not confusion.

We Wrestle not...

God hates mixture because it misrepresents Him. It dilutes truth, it pollutes identity, and it compromises dominion. From Deuteronomy to Revelation, He has made clear: the blend is not blessed.

Identifying Intoxication: A Call to Sobriety

If you find yourself entangled in unequally yoked relationships, seeking someone, anyone, to "touch and agree" with, regardless of alignment...

If you are attempting to live under two professions, one moment claiming to be a sinner, the next professing sainthood...

If you are confused about your identity, tossed between insecurity and spiritual confidence...

You are not just struggling, you are intoxicated.

And the roaring lion is seeking you.

This is not a call to war against the lion.
It is a call to wake up.
To sober up.
To return to the clarity of covenant and the discipline of Kingdom alignment.

"Be sober, be vigilant..." — **1 Peter 5:8 (NKJV)**

Intoxication comes when we drink from Babylon's cup, the golden goblet full of compromise, mixture, and delusion (Revelation 17:4). It dulls discernment, blurs conviction, and opens the door to deception.

You are intoxicated when...

We Wrestle not...

- You trade covenant for convenience, selling what is sacred for a harlot's price, offering your gift, your voice, your calling, to whoever is willing to pay, applaud, or promote.
- You build golden calves out of impatience, forging substitute worship to soothe your fear, because the process of waiting on God costs more than your flesh is willing to pay.
- Your generosity is no longer led by the Spirit, but by guilt, manipulation, emotionalism, or worse, the voice of Mammon masquerading as ministry.
- You mix doctrine to suit your crowd, softening truth to retain influence, replacing conviction with affirmation, and tolerating what you once cast out.
- You measure fruitfulness by reach, not righteousness, counting heads instead of making disciples, aiming for platforms instead of altars.
- You are driven more by likes, shares, and opportunities than by obedience.

This, too, is intoxication.

The Remedy: Sobriety by the Spirit

Sobriety is not self-discipline alone. It is the result of Spirit-filled awareness, a life anchored in truth and covenant:
- Sober living is principled living.
  It honors process. It refuses shortcuts. It walks in agreement.
- Sober speech is covenantal speech.
  It creates life. It reflects Heaven. It doesn't feed devils with idle talk.
- Sober identity is unshakable identity.
  Sons don't wrestle to be accepted. They live from the acceptance of the Beloved.

We Wrestle not...

The roaring lion can only devour what is disoriented, disconnected, and double-minded. But the sober are untouchable, not because they fight harder, but because they stand unmixed, unbending, and unshaken.

In the dark night of the soul, when the lion roars, only the sober will stand.

Imagine a man, heavily intoxicated, walking along a path. A lion roars, and though the lion never attacks, the man stumbles and falls. Not because the lion was stronger, but because the man wasn't sober. The real battle is not against the lion. It's against intoxication.

We are taught, in times of struggle, to fight. We look for demons behind every difficulty. We interpret hardship as attack, and victory as a temporary ceasefire in a spiritual war. But Peter isn't calling us to war, he's calling us to awareness. Not to arm ourselves with swords and declarations, but to stay clear-headed and rooted in truth.

This book isn't written from the perspective of a warfare expert, but from someone who once believed the battle was against the devil rather than against deception.

For years, I waged war.

If money was short, it was the devil. If my relationships were strained, it was a demonic spirit. If my grades dropped, I was under spiritual attack. Every hardship had a supernatural culprit. I was not walking in victory; I was surviving in warfare. My identity was tied to resisting the devil instead of resting in Christ.

My life was framed by what the devil was doing, not what God had already done.

We Wrestle not...

This belief system was deeply embedded in church culture. I enlisted in God's army and went to war, on the streets, in prayer rooms, preaching on the streets at Mardi Gras, shouting declarations, pleading the blood, binding the devil, commanding demons. It was all done with zeal, but little rest.

Looking back, I realize my prayers were shaped more by the fear of the devil than the peace of Christ.

One day, in the middle of my usual warfare prayers, the Lord whispered: *"When are you going to receive what I've done for you?"*

It stunned me. I thought I already had. I was faithful, devoted, on fire. But what He showed me next shifted everything. He wasn't asking me to fight for victory. He was asking me to live from it.

"If then you were raised with Christ, seek those things which are above, where Christ is... Set your mind on things above, not on things on the earth. For you died, and your life is hidden with Christ in God." — **Colossians 3:1–3, NKJV**

In my "secret life with Christ," the devil was not at the center, Jesus was. The warfare mindset that shaped me slowly gave way to a Kingdom mindset. Not of striving, but of ruling. Not of anxiety, but of rest.

I gave up the mixed cup of Babylon and became sober minded. I understood that a roaring lion that couldn't destroy me, was seeking to devour me through deception. When I gave up the mixed drink, of confusion, the instability of double mindedness that makes one unstable left my life for good.

The roar has been silenced, and my stance has become stable.

Conclusion

"The best to deal with the devil is to live in such a way that he is so uncomfortable, he decides to move on." Bishop Gary Clowers (FWCMI)

This is the posture of the believer who no longer lives intoxicated or reactionary.

This is not warfare by declaration, but warfare by demonstration.
- When you walk in righteousness, the accuser has no foothold.
- When you speak the Word with clarity, lies have no landing place.
- When you live as a son, the orphan spirit has no influence.
- When your life becomes too saturated with truth, too guarded by grace, and too yielded to the Spirit, the enemy's best strategy fails, not by confrontation, but by displacement.

"Resist the devil, and he will flee from you." — **James 4:7 (NKJV)**

But resistance is not yelling louder.
Resistance is consistency.
Resistance is sobriety.
Resistance is living in such surrendered sonship that hell has no grip, no gain, and no gateway into your thinking.

Reflection Points

1. According to Peter, what does it mean to be sober in the face of the roaring lion?
2. How does spiritual mixture or religious confusion make believers vulnerable to deception?
3. Why is it easier to blame the devil than examine our own assumptions and doctrines?
4. Have you ever viewed spiritual warfare more as striving than as standing in victory?
5. What would it look like for you to live from the finished work of Christ, not toward it?

CHAPTER FIVE
THE STRATEGY AND THE ARMOR

"For though we walk in the flesh, we do not war after the flesh: (For the weapons of our warfare are not carnal, but mighty through God to the pulling down of strong holds;) Casting down imaginations, and every high thing that exalteth itself against the knowledge of God, and bringing into captivity every thought to the obedience of Christ; And having in a readiness to revenge all disobedience, when your obedience is fulfilled." — **2 Corinthians 10:3–6, KJV**

Strongholds Are Not Demons

The Greek word for stronghold (ochyrōma) describes a fortified mindset, a thought structure built on lies and experiences that resist the truth of God. These are not demons to be exorcised but lies to be exposed. Many live imprisoned by thoughts formed through trauma, religion, or cultural pressure. These mental fortresses hold people captive, not with chains, but with false narratives.

This is the front line of spiritual warfare: not casting out devils but casting down deception.

"Casting down imaginations..." — **2 Corinthians 10:5a**

Imaginations (Greek: logismos) are arguments, reasonings, and speculations, mental blueprints built without God's truth. These imaginations are persuasive. They sound logical. But they exalt themselves against God's Word. They don't submit to truth, they resist it.

We Wrestle not...

The Luciferian Pattern

This resistance to truth is not just abstract, it follows a pattern. It mirrors the rebellion of Lucifer:

"For thou hast said in thine heart, I will ascend into heaven, I will exalt my throne above the stars of God... I will be like the most High." — **Isaiah 14:13–14, KJV**

Pride is the mindset of rebellion. Lucifer's fall began with a thought. And every thought that seeks to dethrone God's truth in our lives follows this same Luciferian pattern. That is the true warfare: confronting the mindsets that refuse to bow.

Capturing Thoughts

"Bringing into captivity every thought to the obedience of Christ..." — **2 Corinthians 10:5b**

This is the real war: not resisting external devils but re-training internal thinking. Thought by thought, belief by belief, we bring them all into alignment with the finished work of Christ.

This is not emotional hype. It's strategic discipline. The believer's warfare is not to gain victory, but to guard faith.

"Fight the good fight of faith..." — **1 Timothy 6:12**

We are never told to fight the devil. The fight is to stay in faith, to continue believing what has already been finished.

We Wrestle not…

Apostolic Career

The weapons of Paul's warfare were not mystical charms or tools of superstitious combat. They were strategic instruments of apostolic engagement, directed at the real battlefield: the minds and belief systems of people.

In 2 Corinthians 10:4, Paul says:

"For the weapons of our warfare are not carnal but mighty in God for pulling down strongholds." — **2 Corinthians 10:4 (NKJV)**

The Greek word translated "warfare" here is στρατεία (strateía), which refers to a military campaign, expedition, or career in service. It's where we get the English word strategy. This is not a word describing random spiritual skirmishes; it refers to a deliberate, organized, mission-driven operation. Paul wasn't describing a chaotic

Battlefield, he was describing his apostolic assignment.

His "warfare" was his apostolic career, a life given to strategically confronting false thinking, overthrowing lies, and establishing truth. Apostles are not merely spiritual figureheads; they are sent ones with a divine commission to reshape the mindsets of people and regions according to the knowledge of Christ.

Wherever Paul went, he identified the dominant thoughts, philosophies, and worldviews of a people, and then intentionally preached, taught, reasoned, and wrote to pull down those strongholds.

The "strongholds" Paul mentions are not spiritual fortresses in the clouds, they are mental and cultural systems of thought. These include religious traditions, pagan philosophies, and internal arguments that resist the truth of the gospel. Paul didn't battle demons; he challenged ideas. He didn't engage in shouting matches with devils; he tore down lies with the truth of Christ.

"Casting down arguments and every high thing that exalts itself against the knowledge of God, bringing every thought into captivity to the obedience of Christ." — **2 Corinthians 10:5 (NKJV)**

This is the true nature of apostolic warfare. Apostles strategically assault deception with revelation, not to gain popularity, but to establish Kingdom order. They confront spiritual chaos not by wrestling spirits, but by bringing divine clarity to confused minds. The apostolic career is not a mystical fight, it is a commissioned campaign of truth.

So when Paul speaks of "warfare," he is describing the entirety of his apostolic function: a lifetime of strategic engagement, armed with the Word of God, driven by the Spirit, and anchored in the mind of Christ. Apostles are reformers, not spiritual mercenaries but master builders, not demon chasers but truth carriers.

Armored to stand

"For we do not wrestle against flesh and blood, but against principalities, against powers...Therefore, take up the whole armor of God, that you may be able to withstand in the evil day, and having done all, to stand." — **Ephesians 6:12–13, NKJV**

Many have interpreted "we wrestle not" as an invitation to spiritual combat. But Paul's message is not warfare-centered, it's identity-centered. The call is not to enter combat but to stand clothed in Christ.

We Wrestle not...

Yes, Paul names principalities and powers. But his focus quickly shifts, not to engage them, but to stand against their deception. Paul clearly states the purpose of the armor is so that we can stand against the wiles or tricks of the devil. Not the devil, his schemes.

Wrestling vs. Standing

Wrestling suggests exposure and struggle. But Paul does not instruct believers to wrestle in the Spirit. Although he acknowledges wrestling, he suggests the alternative made possible by the armor. He tells them to **stand**, armored in Christ.

Those who continually wrestle often do so out of misidentification. But those who know they are hidden in Christ stand in victory. We either wrestle naked of the armor or stand in it!

The Armor Is Christ

Every piece of the armor listed in Ephesians 6 is not just symbolic, it is Christ Himself...

- Belt of Truth — "I am the way, the truth..." **(John 14:6)**
- Breastplate of Righteousness — "Christ is our righteousness..." **(1 Cor. 1:30)**
- Gospel of Peace (Shoes) — *"He Himself is our peace..."* **(Eph. 2:14)**
- Shield of Faith — *"Have faith in God..."* **(Mark 11:22)**
- Helmet of Salvation — *"Author of eternal salvation..."* **(Heb. 5:9)**

We Wrestle not...

- Sword of the Spirit — *"The Word became flesh..."* **(John 1:14)**

To be armored is not to wear a ritualistic suit. It is to put on Christ.

To be armored is to be *"set beyond the conflict into the conquest"* Dr. Rick Kendall (Global Embassy Network)

"For as many of you as were baptized into Christ have put on Christ." — **Galatians 3:27, NKJV**

This is not something you do every morning like brushing your teeth. It's not seasonal or circumstantial. The armor is a permanent spiritual position, because Christ is a permanent Savior. We do not put it on every morning as though we removed it the night before.

We are fit for it and fixed in it.

Hidden in Christ

"For you died, and your life is hidden with Christ in God." — **Colossians 3:3, NKJV**

To be hidden in Christ is to be invisible to the enemy. He doesn't see your flaws; he sees your covering. The enemy doesn't attack what's armored in truth. He targets what's exposed in self-effort.

"Put on the Lord Jesus Christ..." — **Romans 13:14, NKJV**

When we live clothed in Him, we are not wrestling, we are resting. We are not striving, we are standing. To be hidden in Christ is to be clothed in a mystery. Like a knight in full armor, the identity of the believer is no longer outwardly

We Wrestle not...

visible, but entirely concealed within the covering of Christ Himself. The world may see only the exterior, discipline, doctrine, devotion, but what they cannot see is the life that is now hidden with Christ in God.

In the days of medieval warfare, a knight donned his armor not only for protection but for identity. Once encased in metal, he became anonymous, his former name, background, and appearance concealed beneath the polished weight of his armor.

Similarly, the believer, once robed in Christ, becomes a mystery to the world. His past is no longer visible. His sin is no longer remembered. His life is no longer his own. He has put on Christ like armor, and he walks now not in his name but in the name of the King.

The knight's armor was not crafted to display his personality, it was forged to display allegiance. In battle, the knight's identity was not in his face but in the crest on his shield, the colors on his banner, and the cause he served. His personal recognition was secondary, sometimes even irrelevant. What mattered most was that he bore the image, authority, and responsibility of the kingdom he represented.

Likewise, the believer hidden in Christ is not striving for personal visibility, but for faithful representation. Our aim is not to be seen, applauded, or made famous, but to reflect the nature and dominion of the One who clothed us in His righteousness. Our armor is not a platform for self-expression; it is a uniform of surrender, loyalty, and delegated authority.

"We are therefore Christ's ambassadors, as though God were making his appeal through us." — **2 Corinthians 5:20 (NIV)**

We Wrestle not...

The enemy doesn't fear personalities, he fears representatives. He trembles not at the volume of our voice, but at the authority of our alignment. When a believer steps into a situation clothed in Christ, fully armored and surrendered, hell recognizes that the one standing there is not acting on his own but is moving under the seal of another Kingdom.

This is why personal ambition must die when one is truly armored. The knight who cared more about being remembered than representing his King would be unfit for the field. In the same way, Kingdom soldiers are called to decrease, that Christ may increase (John 3:30). We are not building personal brands, we are bearing the banner of the cross, carrying the authority of heaven, and walking under the full endorsement of our sovereign Lord.

So, we seek not for attention, but for allegiance. We speak not for applause, but as ambassadors. And we march not to make a name, but to lift His name, the name of the One in whom we are hidden, armored, and forever covered.

This is how we stand, because we no longer represent who we used to be, "fallen and can't get up". We stand because we are cleansed, made new, and have been given a new identity.

To be fully armored is not to put on things, but to put on a Person. And once that armor is worn, the man inside is no longer vulnerable to accusation or intimidation. He is secure, hidden, and protected, fighting not to gain victory, but from victory already won.

Like a knight whose face is obscured behind a steel visor, the believer's new identity confounds the enemy. Satan can no longer trace the man he used to know. The sinner is gone.

We Wrestle not...

The son now stands in his place. What hell once held in bondage now marches in freedom, covered from head to toe in Christ's triumphant grace.

To be hidden in Christ is to be both unknown and undefeated. The world may mock, misunderstand, or mislabel, but the enemy cannot penetrate what is sealed in the righteousness of God. The believer becomes a holy enigma: walking in divine authority, yet veiled in humility; wielding eternal power yet clothed in peace. He is not who he was. He is who he has become in Him.

The Only Fight: Faith

In all of Scripture, there is only one fight the believer is explicitly commanded to fight: the good fight of faith.

"Fight the good fight of faith, lay hold on eternal life, to which you were also called..." — **1 Timothy 6:12 (NKJV)**

This fight is not with demons or with people. It is a fight to stay persuaded, a struggle to remain anchored in what God has said, even when circumstances scream otherwise. The word "fight" in Greek here is agonízomai, from which we get the English word "agonize." It describes the intensity of a wrestler resisting being overthrown, not by force, but by deception or fatigue.

To fight the good fight of faith means to hold your ground when the enemy offers you a more convenient lie. It means to trust the character of God when your emotions falter. It means to continue believing the Word even when you cannot see results.

We Wrestle not...

The warfare, then, is not one of swords and screaming, it's one of inner resolve. Faith must be fought for, because it is constantly under siege by doubt, delay, and distraction.

The fight of faith is also intricately tied to another command: to labor to enter rest.

"Let us therefore be diligent to enter that rest, lest anyone fall according to the same example of disobedience." — **Hebrews 4:11 (NKJV)**

(Some translations render "be diligent" as "labor" or "make every effort")

This seems paradoxical at first, how do we labor to rest? But in the Kingdom, rest is not the absence of activity; it's the presence of unwavering belief. The Israelites fell in the wilderness not because of giants, but because of unbelief (Hebrews 3:19).

They did not fail to fight, they failed to believe. So, our labor is not physical, it is the strenuous spiritual discipline of staying rooted in trust. We wrestle to remain in the posture of rest, the settled confidence that God is who He says He is and will do what He promised.

This kind of rest is only accessible by faith. It is not passive resignation but active agreement with God's Word. It's what Jesus demonstrated when He slept in the storm while the disciples panicked.

His rest was not apathy, it was authority.

He was so rooted in the Father's word that chaos couldn't move Him. That's the rest we labor to enter: the place where fear, striving, and performance end, and faith rules.

We Wrestle not...

And because faith is the only fight, we're called to engage in, it reveals that our battle is not for victory, but from victory. We are not trying to win what Christ already won; we are believing in and enforcing His triumph. Every command to stand (Ephesians 6:13), every call to resist (James 4:7), and every instruction to endure (Hebrews 10:35–36) is ultimately about staying convinced of what Christ has done, who we are in Him, and what He has promised.

Closing Declaration

I am hidden in Christ, clothed not in fear, but in full armor. I am not fighting for victory; I am fighting to stay persuaded. I reject the lies of the enemy and silence every voice that exalts itself against the knowledge of my God. I put on Christ, not for recognition, but for representation. My life is not my own, I carry the banner of a greater Kingdom.

I do not wrestle with shadows or chase after defeated foes. I cast down imaginations. I demolish arguments. I take every thought captive. I am an ambassador, not a victim. A son, not a slave. A builder, not a brawler.

I fight the good fight of faith. I labor to enter His rest. I war by believing. I stand by trusting. I overcome by truth. My armor is not for display, it is for dominion. The mystery of who I am is sealed in who He is.

I have been authorized, assigned, and anointed.
No weapon formed against me shall prosper.
No thought shall rule me but the mind of Christ.
No voice shall move me but the voice of my Father.

We Wrestle not…

I am fully armored.
I am divinely aligned.
I am dangerously persuaded.
And I will not be moved.

We Wrestle not…

Reflection & Discussion

1. What are some examples of strongholds in your own thinking that need to be confronted with truth?
2. How does understanding the mind as the battlefield change your approach to spiritual warfare?
3. In what ways have you "wrestled" when you should have simply stood?
Have you viewed the armor of God as something to "put on" daily, or as your permanent position in Christ?
4. How can you intentionally remain hidden in Christ while fighting the good fight of faith?

CHAPTER SIX
THE HISTORY OF SPIRITUAL WARFARE

How the Church Drifted from Apostolic Victory to Modern Mysticism

A CALL TO RECOVER THE KINGDOM LENS:

As we trace the long and winding path from the apostles to the apostles of today, one reality becomes evident: spiritual warfare has shifted from being a matter of inner transformation and identity in Christ to a system of external combat and mystical confrontation.

The early Church understood the battleground as the human heart, and the enemy as anything that exalted itself against the knowledge of God. The strategy was not assault but abiding. Not mapping demons, but maturing sons. Not screaming into the air, but standing in truth.

But today, the Church is often distracted, marching under the banner of warfare but forgetting the One who already won. We have built elaborate doctrines around darkness, while the Gospel commands us to walk in the light. We have trained believers to look for devils instead of look to Jesus. In doing so, we've left our seated place in heavenly authority and returned to the trenches as if Christ never triumphed. Yet a remnant still remembers.

A remnant is awakening to the fact that Jesus is not competing with darkness, He reigns over it. The Gospel of the Kingdom is not a battle plan, it is a proclamation:

We Wrestle not...

"All authority has been given to Me in heaven and on earth." **(Matthew 28:18, NKJV)'**

So let this chapter not merely inform, but reform. Let it remind us that we are not wrestling for dominion, we are reigning from it. That we are not waiting for victory, we are walking in it. That the true battlefield is belief, and our fight is the good fight of faith.

It's time to come out of the trenches and take our seat at the right hand of the Father.

It's time to recover the Kingdom lens.

The Language of Conflict: When Terms Collide

Part of the confusion in modern theology stems from the phrase itself: spiritual warfare. These two words, when rightly defined, each hold weight and clarity in Scripture.

Spiritual: refers to that which is of the Spirit, invisible but eternal, divine in origin or demonic in distortion.

Warfare: speaks to conflict, struggle, or confrontation.

But when these words are joined without precision, they often become a breeding ground for theological dualism, which is the idea that light and darkness are in equal opposition, locked in an eternal struggle for dominance. This is not the Gospel. God has no rival. Christ has already conquered. The Holy Spirit does not wrestle with demons; He displaces them.

"Spiritual warfare" as a term has, in many circles, collapsed into a catch-all that justifies fear, fosters superstition, and shifts focus away from Christ's finished work. It too easily becomes an excuse for ongoing struggle rather than an invitation to rest, reign, and renew the mind.

When believers adopt this undefined, hybrid language, they unintentionally conflate the internal conflict of belief with external enemies of flesh and blood. They blur the line between resisting temptation and battling geography. And they forget that Christ is seated, not striving, and we are seated with Him.

A Historical Pathway of Spiritual Warfare Doctrine

From the victorious proclamation of Christ's triumph in the early Church to the fear-laden and territorial strategies of modern warfare theology, this chapter traces the path of descent. It reveals how, over centuries, the Church drifted away from the Gospel of the Kingdom into frameworks shaped more by fear of the devil than by faith in Christ's finished work. What began as a Christ-centered confidence in the believer's identity and authority has been rebranded into battle cries against imagined foes, territorial spirits, and endless "strategic" campaigns.

The apostolic foundation: Victory in Christ

The apostolic foundation of the early Church was not just Christ-centered, it was cross-centered and resurrection-anchored, meaning it viewed Satan as already defeated, not merely resisted. Their model did not include binding spirits or territorial warfare but instead declared and demonstrated the triumph of Christ. Here are several foundational points the early Church embraced that reflected this Kingdom reality:

We Wrestle not...

Christ's Victory Over the Devil Was Final and Public

"Having disarmed principalities and powers, He made a public spectacle of them, triumphing over them in it." — **Colossians 2:15 (NKJV)**

Foundation:
The early Church believed that at the cross, Jesus stripped Satan and all spiritual authorities of their power. The battle was not ongoing, it was finished. The Church's job was to announce this victory, not re-fight it.

Believers Are Seated with Christ in Heavenly Places

"And raised us up together and made us sit together in the heavenly places in Christ Jesus." — **Ephesians 2:6 (NKJV)**

Foundation:
Spiritual warfare, as the apostles saw it, began from a throne, not a battlefield. The early Church taught believers that their position in Christ meant authority over darkness, not vulnerability to it.

The Devil Has No Legal Access to the Redeemed

"He has delivered us from the power of darkness and conveyed us into the kingdom of the Son of His love." — **Colossians 1:13 (NKJV)**

Foundation:
There was a clear understanding that salvation translated believers into a new domain. Darkness had no dominion over them. The enemy's only weapon was deception, and even that could be broken by truth.

We Wrestle not...

The Gospel Itself Is the Weapon Against Darkness

"To open their eyes, in order to turn them from darkness to light, and from the power of Satan to God..." — **Acts 26:18 (NKJV)**

Foundation:
The apostolic commission was not about confronting demons but proclaiming truth. Evangelism was seen as warfare because light expelled darkness simply by being preached. Apostles did not rebuke regional spirits, they preached the Gospel and watched strongholds fall.

The Church Had Authority to Cast Out Demons, Not Entertain Them

"In My name they will cast out demons..." — **Mark 16:17 (NKJV)**

"Come out of her!" — **Acts 16:18**

Foundation:
Deliverance, when needed, was direct and decisive. There were no long rituals, no mappings, and no fear. It was a clear demonstration of Christ's authority, not a wrestling match. The early Church saw demons as defeated foes, not powerful adversaries.

The Early Church Did Not Teach Warfare Rituals or Strategies

Evidence:
There are no apostolic instructions in Acts or the Epistles on how to:
- Bind territorial spirits

We Wrestle not...

- Anoint locations
- Map strongholds
- Break generational curses

Foundation:
The silence of Scripture on these popular modern practices is itself a powerful reflection of the apostolic model. Their focus was always on Christ, the Kingdom, and transformation of hearts, not battling devils in the atmosphere.

The Armor of God Was Positional, Not Offensive Against Devils

"Put on the whole armor of God... that you may be able to stand." — **Ephesians 6:11 (NKJV)**

Foundation:
The armor of God wasn't given for us to go hunting spirits; it was to stand in truth. Each piece reflects a gospel reality, a Christ identity, not a weapon to hurl at the devil. The early Church understood spiritual conflict as holding ground already won, not taking ground from the enemy.

Summary

The early Church's foundation was:
- Christ has already won.
- Believers are in Him.
- Satan is beneath them.
- Truth is their greatest weapon.
- The Gospel is their primary strategy.

They did not fear deception, elevate demons, or emphasize mystical warfare strategies. Instead, they preached, healed,

We Wrestle not...

taught, baptized, and walked in the authority of a finished work.

The early Church did not have a theology of territorial spirits as we see in modern spiritual warfare teachings. The idea that certain demons or principalities are assigned to geographical areas, and must be identified, mapped, and overthrown by prayer or prophetic acts, is entirely absent from the New Testament and early Church practice.

Here's a breakdown of the early Church's position by absence and contrast:

No Apostolic Teaching on Territorial Spirits

There is no record in Acts or the Epistles where the apostles:
- Identified spirits over cities or nations
- Prayed against regional demonic powers
- Conducted "spiritual mapping"
- Engaged in "strategic-level warfare" to dislodge demonic rulers

Instead, they preached the Gospel, healed the sick, planted churches, and taught sound doctrine.

Paul in Athens (Acts 17): He encountered a city "given to idols," yet he didn't bind the spirit of idolatry, he preached the resurrection of Jesus.

Paul in Ephesus (Acts 19): A city known for magic and the occult. Paul never confronted the "spirit over Ephesus", he taught the Word for two years, and the people themselves burned their occult books.

Principalities and Powers Were Viewed as Defeated, Not Engaged

"...Having disarmed principalities and powers, He made a public spectacle of them, triumphing over them in it." — **Colossians 2:15 (NKJV)**

The early Church viewed principalities and powers as disarmed. They were acknowledged (Ephesians 6:12), but not engaged with, instead, believers were told to stand, resist deception, and live in Christ's authority.

Evangelism Was the Apostolic Weapon Against Darkness

"To open their eyes... to turn them from darkness to light, and from the power of Satan to God..." — **Acts 26:18 (NKJV)**

The early Church believed that preaching the truth displaced demonic influence. They didn't attempt to cleanse cities through intercession, they colonized them with the Gospel.

Strongholds Were Mental, Not Geographical

"...pulling down strongholds, casting down arguments and every high thing that exalts itself against the knowledge of God..." — **2 Corinthians 10:4–5 (NKJV)**

Paul defined strongholds as patterns of thought, not spirits over territories. The battlefield was the mind, and the weapon was truth, not territorial confrontation.

We Wrestle not...

Early Church Fathers Never Taught Territorial Warfare

Writings of early Fathers like Ignatius, Justin Martyr, Irenaeus, and Tertullian make no mention of territorial spirits or methods to battle them. They confronted false doctrine, heresies, and idolatry through teaching and martyrdom, not mystical warfare.

Summary: The Early Church's Position on Territorial Spirits

- They acknowledged demonic influence in cultures and individuals, but did not personify or name "regional demons."
- They never engaged spirits over cities, nor instructed churches to do so.
- They overcame darkness by discipling nations, not by binding devils.
- They trusted the Gospel, not warfare rituals, to shift spiritual climates.

Conclusion:

The idea of territorial spirits comes not from Scripture.

What Was the Early Church's Position on Territorial Spirits?

The early Church had no theology, strategy, or practice regarding territorial spirits. They did not believe they needed to confront demons over cities or nations. Instead, they preached Christ, established the Church, and trusted the power of the Gospel to displace darkness.

We Wrestle not…

They Did Not Name or Bind Spirits Over Regions

There is no biblical or historical record of early believers or apostles:

- Naming spirits over cities (e.g., "spirit of Athens," "principality over Rome")
- Binding or casting down regional demons
- Conducting spiritual mapping or territorial cleansing

Even in Ephesus, a center of demonic activity and idolatry (Acts 19), Paul never addressed a territorial spirit, he simply preached the Word, and the people turned from darkness voluntarily. **The culture shifted because the hearts changed.**

They Acknowledged Principalities, But Did Not Engage Them

"Having disarmed principalities and powers…" — **Colossians 2:15 (NKJV)**

Principalities were real, but they were already disarmed by Christ. The believer's posture was standing in truth, not fighting devils in the sky. Paul never instructed the church to "rebuke spirits over Ephesus or Corinth", he told them to renew their minds, walk in holiness, and stand firm in faith.

Evangelism and Discipleship were the order of the early church

"To open their eyes, to turn them from darkness to light…" — **Acts 26:18 (NKJV)**

We Wrestle not...

The early Church changed spiritual climates by changing minds through truth.
- No prayer walks.
- No prophetic acts on high places.
- No exorcism of city gates.

They planted churches, preached Jesus, and taught sound doctrine.

Early Church Fathers Never Mentioned Territorial Spirits

Church Fathers like:
- Ignatius of Antioch
- Justin Martyr
- Irenaeus
- Tertullian
- Origen

...wrote extensively on spiritual conflict, martyrdom, heresy, and paganism, yet never referenced spirits ruling over cities or nations. The warfare they described was:
- Cultural (against idolatry and immorality)
- Doctrinal (against false teaching)
- Moral (against sin)

They saw darkness as something displaced by truth, not something to be wrestled with in the air.

We Wrestle not...

Territorial Spirits Is a Modern Invention

The idea of demons ruling over geography, requiring strategic warfare to dislodge them, comes not from Scripture but from:
- 20th-century spiritual warfare movements
- Influences like C. Peter Wagner, George Otis Jr., and John Dawson
- Misapplication of Daniel 10 and Ephesians 6

This teaching blends spiritual fear with mystical activism and shifts focus from Christ's finished work to human-driven confrontation.

Final Kingdom Perspective:

The early Church didn't cast out spirits over cities, they cast down lies in people's hearts.
They didn't war with demons in the air, they preached the Kingdom on the ground.
They didn't identify principalities, they magnified the Prince of Peace.

Athanasius of Alexandria (c. 296–373)

One of the most influential early Church Fathers, did address spiritual conflict, but his perspective on spiritual warfare was profoundly different from modern interpretations.

Rather than describing warfare as external combat with demons, Athanasius viewed it as a spiritual and moral struggle for holiness, centered on union with Christ, the victory of the cross, and the transformation of the believer. His most vivid treatment of the topic appears in his biography of St. Antony the Great titled *The Life of Antony*, which became foundational for early Christian monasticism (a solitary choice of lifestyle away from ordinary society), and theology on spiritual conflict.

A look at a detailed summary of Athanasius's in-depth perspective on spiritual warfare, drawn from *The Life of Antony*, his theological works, and letters.

ATHANASIUS'S IN-DEPTH PERSPECTIVE ON SPIRITUAL WARFARE

Christ's Incarnation and Cross Disarmed Demonic Power

Athanasius taught that the incarnation of Christ marked the decisive turning point in the war against Satan.

"The Savior's advent in the flesh meant the immediate fall of the demonic powers... No longer do demons speak through oracles, no longer are charms effective."
— **On the Incarnation, §47 (De Incarnatione Verbi Dei ("On the Incarnation of the Word of God) Written 318-335 AD**

Perspective:
The power of the devil was already broken by the coming of Christ. Spiritual warfare was not about defeating Satan again, it was about standing in the reality of Christ's victory and refusing to be drawn back into deception.

The Battle Is Internal, Between the Flesh and the Spirit

Athanasius, through Antony's example, emphasized that warfare is primarily internal, a struggle to resist the passions, temptations, and deceptions that seek to draw the soul away from God.

"The demons, being cowards, pretend and make displays, but are easily driven away by a firm soul and by faith in God."
— Life of Antony, §30 Biography of Antony the Great written by Athanasius of Alexandria 356 AD

Perspective:
Spiritual warfare is not about binding demons in the air, but disciplining the soul, overcoming pride, lust, and fear, and learning to abide in prayer, humility, and Scripture. The demons only gain influence when the believer gives them ground through fleshly indulgence or fear.

Demons Use Fear, Illusion, and Suggestion, Not Power

Athanasius made it clear that demons do not have inherent authority or power over the believer. Their primary weapons are lies, illusions, and fear, similar to Paul's teaching on "arguments and high things that exalt themselves against the knowledge of God" (2 Corinthians 10:4–5).

"The demons are deceivers and behave in this way in order to frighten monks; but one should not fear their displays."
— Life of Antony, §35 Biography of Antony the Great written by Athanasius of Alexandria 356 AD

Perspective:
True warfare is about discerning and rejecting fear, not engaging in conflict. Antony's strength lay in his peace, joy, and anchored identity in Christ, not in shouting or rituals.

We Wrestle not...

The Word of God and the Name of Jesus Are the Weapons

Athanasius shows Antony repeatedly using Scripture, the sign of the cross, and the name of Jesus to overcome demonic oppression.

"Antony armed himself with faith, the sign of the cross, and the words of Scripture."
— ***Life of Antony, §43 Biography of Antony the Great written by Athanasius of Alexandria 356 AD***

Perspective:
Victory is maintained through Christ-centered devotion, not mystical techniques. There's no mention of strategic mapping, territorial binding, or special prayers, just abiding faith, ascetic discipline, and the Word.

The Cross Makes the Devil Powerless

Athanasius returns often to the idea that Satan has already been defeated. The demonic realm trembles at the name and cross of Christ, not because of magical properties, but because they are signs of irreversible defeat.

"By the sign of the cross, and by the name of Jesus, all the illusions of the devil are brought to nothing."
— ***Life of Antony, §65 Biography of Antony the Great written by Athanasius of Alexandria 356 AD***

Perspective:
Spiritual warfare is not about trying to win a fight, but about remaining aligned with the One who already won. Peace, not panic, is the fruit of victory.

We Wrestle not…

Warfare Is About Sanctification, Not Confrontation

Athanasius portrays spiritual conflict as a necessary path to holiness, not a ministry of rebuking demons. Antony did not seek out confrontation. Instead, demons came to resist his pursuit of God, but he overcame them by virtue, prayer, and Scripture.

"It is not our duty to flee temptation but to endure and grow strong by the grace of God."
*— **Life of Antony, §28 Biography of Antony the Great written by Athanasius of Alexandria 356 AD***

Perspective:
Spiritual warfare is not a separate "ministry"; it is the byproduct of sanctification. When the believer draws near to God, resistance comes, but victory is already assured.

Athanasius's View vs. Modern Warfare Teaching

Athanasius	Modern Spiritual Warfare
Internal battle against passions	External battle against demons
Victory through Christ's cross	Warfare to reclaim victory
Fear and deception are demonic tools	Demons viewed as territorial rulers
Word of God and prayer as weapons	Mapping, naming spirits, aggressive rituals
Sanctification through suffering	Confrontation through authority
Warfare is part of devotion	Warfare is often a specialized ministry

Conclusion on Athanasius

Athanasius's spiritual warfare was cross-shaped, Scripture-saturated, and peace-filled. He taught that demons are defeated, deceptive, and terrified of the light. The believer is not to fear them, chase them, or center their life around them. Warfare is simply the resistance that comes when the Kingdom of God breaks into the soul.

Augustine of Hippo (354–430)

Augustine offered one of the most enduring theological perspectives on spiritual warfare. Unlike modern teachings focused on external combat with demons, Augustine emphasized the battle within, the struggle between the will and sin, between the *City of God and the City of Man*.

Spiritual Warfare is Primarily an Internal Battle with Sin and the Flesh

Augustine believed that the true battlefield is within the human soul, where disordered loves and sinful desires wage war against the will of God. Spiritual warfare was about conversion and transformation, not demon-hunting.

"I was in conflict with myself... The enemy was within my own soul." — **Confessions, Book 8**

Satan is Real but Subordinate to God's Sovereignty

Augustine acknowledged the existence of Satan but insisted that he operates only under God's permission.

We Wrestle not...

"The devil is like a chained dog; he can bark, but he cannot bite unless God permits." — **City of God, Book 22**

The City of God vs. the City of Man

Spiritual warfare, for Augustine, was the historical and spiritual conflict between the City of God (those who love God) and the City of Man (those who love self). This was not about territories but about the allegiance of the heart.

Grace is the Ultimate Weapon

Augustine believed victory was not achieved by human effort or spiritual techniques but through God's sovereign grace.

"Give what You command, and command what You will."
— **Confessions, Book 10**

The Armor of God is the Life of Christ in the Believer

For Augustine, putting on the 'armor of God' meant putting on Christ, living a life of truth, righteousness, and faith.

"The whole armor of God is Christ. Put Him on, and you will stand."

Deliverance Comes Through Sacraments, Scripture, and Community

Deliverance from spiritual bondage, according to Augustine, came through the means of grace: Baptism, the Eucharist, Scripture, and the community of faith.

We Wrestle not...

Fear of the Devil is Evidence of Weak Faith

Augustine taught that Christians should fear sin more than Satan. Obsessing over demonic power showed a lack of confidence in God's sovereignty.

"The devil can tempt, but he cannot force. What power does he have over you unless you yield?"

Spiritual warfare, in Augustine's conversion story, is about the liberation of the will by the grace of God, not the binding of a devil but the breaking of self.

Augustine's Spiritual Warfare Framework

Theme	Augustine's Perspective
Source of conflict	Internal: the will, disordered desires
Satan's role	Real, but limited and subordinate
Battlefield	The heart (City of God vs. City of Man)
Victory strategy	Grace, not striving
Spiritual armor	A life formed in Christ
Deliverance means	Word, Sacrament, Church
View of fear	Fear empowers temptation, not protection

We Wrestle not...

The War Within: Monastic Traditions on Spiritual Conflict

The early monastic tradition, beginning in the deserts of Egypt and later forming structured communities in the West, held a profound perspective on spiritual warfare. Rather than external battles with demons, monastic thinkers focused on the 'war within', the inner conflict of the soul against passion, distraction, and pride.

Foundational voices from that tradition and their contributions to the theology of inner spiritual warfare.

Evagrius Ponticus (345–399)

Evagrius was a desert monk who outlined the psychology of temptation. He identified 'eight evil thoughts' (which later became the Seven Deadly Sins), including gluttony, lust, greed, sadness, anger, acedia (spiritual sloth), vainglory, and pride.

Evagrius taught that demons tempt by attacking the mind through thoughts and imaginations. The solution, he said, was watchfulness (Greek: nepsis), prayer, and meditating on Scripture. For Evagrius, spiritual warfare was about mastering thoughts and guarding the heart.

John Cassian (360–435)

A student of the desert fathers, Cassian preserved and expanded on Evagrius' teachings. In his works *'Conferences' and 'Institutes,'* he described how monks battled interior temptations. Cassian emphasized the importance of discernment, understanding where thoughts came from, and how to respond.

We Wrestle not...

He did not advocate rebuking demons, but rather, cultivating inner stillness and obedience. Warfare, for Cassian, was a matter of long obedience in the same direction.

Benedict of Nursia (480–547)

Known for his *'Rule of Saint Benedict,'* he structured communal monastic life around prayer, work, and obedience. For Benedict, spiritual warfare was about humility, daily discipline, and stability. The monk's enemy was not only temptation, but distraction, pride, and disobedience.

The weapons were rhythm, repetition, and surrender. His famous call was: 'Listen, my son, to the teaching of a master...'

Other Contributors

Gregory the Great (540–604) emphasized the battle between virtues and vices in his *'Moralia on Job.'* Isaac of Nineveh (7th century) focused on tears, silence, and divine mercy as weapons in the unseen struggle. These writers agreed: spiritual warfare is not a theater of shouting at demons, but a slow sanctification of the soul.

Conclusion

The monastic tradition taught that the greatest warfare is waged in the heart. Lust, pride, anger, and despair are more dangerous than any demon in the air. These fathers left a legacy not of fear but of formation, a roadmap of humility, prayer, fasting, and inner stillness. Their warfare was not aggressive, it was contemplative, Christ-centered, and victorious through death to self.

Martin Luther (Reformer) on Spiritual Warfare

Martin Luther (1483–1546), the leader of the Protestant Reformation, offered a bold and Gospel-centered view of spiritual warfare. For Luther, the battleground was not the sky but the soul, particularly the conscience, where Satan accused, the Law condemned, and grace triumphed. His break from the Roman Catholic Church was not only theological but spiritual, as he saw the Reformation as a war for truth and freedom.

The True Battlefield: Conscience and Condemnation

Luther taught that Satan's primary weapon was accusation, using guilt and shame to lead the believer into despair. The war was internal. The conscience, burdened by sin, could only be liberated by the Gospel.

"The devil's greatest work is to accuse and condemn the conscience so that we despair of God's mercy." — **Lectures on Galatians**

Satan as the Accuser, Not an Omnipresent Enemy

While Luther acknowledged Satan's activity, he emphasized that the devil is a defeated liar who can only threaten but not destroy. The believer's response was not fear, but faith in Christ's atonement.

"When the devil throws our sins up to us... I know One who suffered and made satisfaction on my behalf."

We Wrestle not...

The Word of God as the Ultimate Weapon

For Luther, the Word of God was the supreme weapon in warfare. No ritual or incantation compared to the power of the Gospel.

"One little word shall fell him." — **A Mighty Fortress Is Our God**

Prayer and Hymns as Forms of Warfare

Luther believed prayer and worship were powerful means of warfare, not to bind demons, but to strengthen faith and glorify God. Victory came through proclaiming truth louder than lies.

Reformation Itself Was Spiritual Warfare

Luther viewed the Roman Catholic Church's teachings as spiritual bondage, keeping people from the truth of grace. He called the Reformation a divine rescue from deception and fear.

"The Papacy is the kingdom of the devil, and the Pope is his apostle." — **Against the Roman Papacy**

Luther's Spiritual Warfare Perspective

Theme	Luther's Perspective
Battlefield	The conscience (accusation vs. grace)
Enemy	Satan the accuser, not omnipotent

Weapon	The Word of God
Strategy	Faith in justification through Christ
Prayer	A cry of trust, not a tactic
Worship	Proclamation of victory
Reformation	Liberation from religious deception and fear

Modern era: Rise of the warfare industry

Jessie Penn-Lewis (1861–1927)

Author of *'War on the Saints'*, Penn-Lewis introduced the idea of demonic infiltration in the mind, promoting extreme vigilance and introspection. Though influential, her ideas contributed to *fear-based thinking*, often suggesting the devil was behind every thought or spiritual experience.

Key Aspects of Jessie Penn-Lewis's View on Spiritual Warfare:

High Emphasis on Spiritual Deception
- Penn-Lewis believed that after spiritual experiences (especially those involving revival or intense manifestations), believers were uniquely vulnerable to demonic counterfeits.
- Her central concern was that Satan could impersonate the Holy Spirit and influence the mind, emotions, or body of even sincere Christians.

We Wrestle not...

Watchfulness Over the Mind, but Not in a Pauline Sense
- While she addressed the mind extensively, her framework was not grounded in renewing the mind through truth, as Paul wrote in Romans 12:2 or 2 Corinthians 10:4-5.
- Instead, she viewed the mind as a battleground vulnerable to deception, and called believers to be suspicious of thoughts, impressions, and spiritual experiences, always questioning their source.
- Her counsel focused on watching for demonic intrusion, often leaning more into fear than transformation.

Spiritual Warfare as a Defensive Posture
- Penn-Lewis emphasized self-examination, rejection of experiences that could be false, and constant vigilance, more defensive than triumphant.
- She encouraged prayers of renunciation and denouncement of false spiritual influences, practices that became foundational to later spiritual warfare models but were not present in apostolic teaching.

A Mixture That Influenced Modern Teachings
- Her ideas were deeply influential in shaping the fear-based, introspective, and suspicious lens that later defined many spiritual warfare teachings in charismatic and deliverance movements.
- While she did believe in submission to Christ, and referenced the cross as the solution to deception, her actual focus was often on discerning demons rather than renewing the mind with truth.

Jessie Penn-Lewis did not consider renewing the mind (in the biblical sense) to be the greatest form of warfare. Her teachings emphasized:

We Wrestle not...

- Vigilance against deception
- Rejection of supernatural experiences without discernment
- Suspicion of the mind's impressions
- A defensive posture rather than a victorious one

Her theology was a mixture, grounded in personal holiness and discernment, but deeply influenced by fear of spiritual infiltration. She laid the groundwork for modern spiritual warfare doctrines centered on binding spirits, rejecting thoughts, and questioning spiritual manifestations, rather than the transformative power of truth, sonship, and renewal.

A Kingdom perspective of the Four Core Principles of Jessie Penn-Lewis's Warfare Model

Satan Can Deceive the Spiritually Sincere

Penn-Lewis taught that those who are zealous for God, especially those experiencing revival or deep spiritual experiences, are the most vulnerable to demonic deception.

Kingdom Counterpoint:

"My sheep hear My voice, and I know them, and they follow Me." — **John 10:27 (NKJV)**

"You were sealed with the Holy Spirit of promise..." — **Ephesians 1:13 (NKJV)**

The New Covenant teaches that sons are not led by suspicion but by the Spirit (Romans 8:14). While discernment is necessary, Penn-Lewis framed spiritual sensitivity as a liability rather than a gift. Jesus does not say His sheep might hear strange voices and need to test them every moment, He says they hear His voice.

Evil Spirits Can Imitate the Holy Spirit's Operations

She warned that demons could mimic prophecy, tongues, healing, and spiritual leadings, especially in revival environments.

Kingdom Counterpoint:

"Every good gift and every perfect gift is from above..." — **James 1:17 (NKJV)**

"The anointing which you have received... teaches you concerning all things... and is not a lie." — **1 John 2:27 (NKJV)**

The idea that demons can so closely impersonate the Holy Spirit that believers must constantly second-guess their spiritual experiences is contrary to the confidence Scripture gives. The Holy Spirit is not fragile, and He does not operate in confusion.

We are told to test the spirits, yes, but through truth and fruit, not fear and paralysis.

The Mind and Emotions Are Primary Gateways for Demonic Influence

Penn-Lewis emphasized that a believer's thoughts, feelings, and even mental impressions could become doorways for spiritual deception.

Kingdom Counterpoint:

"Be transformed by the renewing of your mind..." — **Romans 12:2 (NKJV)**

"You have the mind of Christ." — **1 Corinthians 2:16 (NKJV)**

Scripture does not tell believers to fear their mind, it tells them to renew it. The Holy Spirit renews the inner man day by day (2 Corinthians 4:16). The mind is not the battleground for demons to gain entry, it is the place where the truth sets us free (John 8:32). Her teaching reduced the mind to a threat rather than a vessel for transformation.

All Spiritual Experiences Must Be Suspect Until Proven Pure

She taught that believers must analyze, question, and often reject supernatural experiences unless rigorously proven to be from God.

Kingdom Counterpoint:

"Do not quench the Spirit. Do not despise prophecies. Test all things; hold fast what is good." — **1 Thessalonians 5:19–21 (NKJV)**

"Where the Spirit of the Lord is, there is liberty." — **2 Corinthians 3:17 (NKJV)**

Penn-Lewis's framework promotes paralysis by analysis. It is built on fear of deception, not freedom in Christ. While the Bible encourages testing, it never commands suspicion as a lifestyle. We are to hold fast what is good, not reject everything until proven otherwise.

Spiritual Warfare Is a Defensive Posture of Constant Guarding

Her model promoted a posture of retreat, watching, renouncing, and continual self-examination.

Kingdom Counterpoint:

"And raised us up together, and made us sit together in the heavenly places in Christ Jesus." — **Ephesians 2:6 (NKJV)**

"Having disarmed principalities and powers, He made a public spectacle of them..." — **Colossians 2:15 (NKJV)**

"Fight the good fight of faith..." — **1 Timothy 6:12 (NKJV)**

The only fight we are called to fight is the fight of faith, not the fight against devils. True warfare is believing, standing, and resting in the authority and victory of Christ. Spiritual warfare is not a lifelong retreat into suspicion; it is the bold advance of sons in the Kingdom. We don't fight to win, we stand in victory.

Her Model Promotes Fear Over Faith

Jessie Penn-Lewis sincerely desired to protect believers from deception, but her model lacks a victorious, Kingdom-based foundation. It subtly empowers the devil with access and influence over the redeemed that Scripture does not support. It places suspicion where Scripture places assurance, and fear where Christ placed freedom.

Watchman Nee (1903–1972)

In The Spiritual Man and other works, Nee developed a model of warfare tied to the tripartite nature of man, spirit, soul, and body. He warned of *soul-power* and demonic influence, and although he pointed to Christ's victory, his writings opened the door to a more mystical, psychological approach to warfare.

Watchman Nee warned against the operation of familiar spirits working in the soul, often disguising themselves as gifts of the Spirit. His concern was rooted in his broader teaching on the tripartite nature of man, spirit, soul, and body, and the potential for the soulish realm (mind, will, emotions) to become a gateway for deceptive spiritual experiences if the believer is not properly discerning.

Watchman Nee's Warning in Context

In books like *The Spiritual Man* and *The Latent Power of the Soul*, Nee makes the following points:

1. The Human Soul Can Be Powerful, but Dangerous:
Nee believed that when a believer lives from the soul rather than the spirit, they become vulnerable to spiritual deception. The soul can mimic spiritual experiences, and this can open the door to demonic influence.

2. Familiar Spirits Mimic the Holy Spirit:
Nee warned that familiar spirits (demonic entities that imitate divine activity) can operate through emotionally charged or unsubmitted believers and even mimic

supernatural gifts like prophecy, tongues, and healing. He was deeply concerned about manifestations that had no true cross-bearing, no death to self, and no root in the Word.

3. False Gifts and Experiences:
He emphasized that some manifestations attributed to the Holy Spirit might, in fact, be soulish or demonic in origin, especially if they bypass the discernment of the spirit and appeal to the flesh or emotionalism.

Biblical Precedents for Nee's Concerns

The Bible does, in fact, support the possibility of deception through false spiritual manifestations, and offers several warnings:

Familiar Spirits
- Leviticus 20:6 (NKJV) – "And the person who turns to mediums and familiar spirits… I will set My face against that person…"
- These spirits impersonate the dead or divine messengers and were explicitly forbidden under Mosaic law.

False Signs and Wonders
- 2 Thessalonians 2:9–10 (NKJV) – "The coming of the lawless one is according to the working of Satan, with all power, signs, and lying wonders…"
- This speaks to counterfeit miracles that deceive those not grounded in truth.

False Prophets and Deceiving Spirits
- Timothy 4:1 (NKJV) – "Now the Spirit expressly says that in latter times some will depart from the

faith, giving heed to deceiving spirits and doctrines of demons."
- Matthew 7:22–23 – Jesus rejects those who claimed to prophesy, cast out demons, and perform wonders in His name.

Simon the Sorcerer (Acts 8:9–24)
- Simon amazed people with supernatural acts, but his heart was not right before God, showing that not all spiritual displays are of the Holy Spirit.

The Slave Girl with a Spirit of Divination (Acts 16:16–18)
- This girl followed Paul, proclaiming true things, yet Paul discerned it was a spirit of divination (Greek: python), and cast it out.

These biblical references are vitally important but can only be understood when looking at them through a Kingdom lens.

The Fear of Deception: A Modern Insecurity, Not a Kingdom Mindset

While Watchman Nee was deeply sincere in his desire for believers to walk in purity and discernment, his teachings on familiar spirits and soulish manifestations created a doorway for fear-based interpretations of the supernatural. Over time, his warnings were adopted and expanded by others into entire doctrines of spiritual warfare based on suspicion, self-examination, and the idea that believers must guard themselves constantly from demonic infiltration, even through the gifts of the Spirit.

We Wrestle not...

But is this concern biblically justified?

Let's examine five of the most cited "supporting scriptures" used to validate fear-driven discernment and show how each, when read through the lens of the finished work of Christ, strengthens the case against modern spiritual warfare teachings.

Leviticus 20:6 – The Willful Turn to Mediums

"And the person who turns to mediums and familiar spirits, to prostitute himself with them, I will set My face against that person..." — **Leviticus 20:6, NKJV**

This passage deals with willful defilement under the Law. It speaks of those who knowingly and deliberately seek out mediums. But believers in Christ are not under the Law (Romans 6:14). The blood of Jesus has destroyed the works of the devil (1 John 3:8) and rendered the legal code obsolete by fulfilling it in us (Romans 8:4).

The fear that a born-again, Spirit-sealed believer might be unknowingly "entertaining a familiar spirit" undermines the sufficiency of the cross and the seal of the Holy Spirit.

2 Thessalonians 2:9–10 – Lying Signs and Wonders

"...with all power, signs, and lying wonders..." — **2 Thessalonians 2:9, NKJV**

Paul is not warning about believers *accidentally* being deceived by spiritual gifts. He is addressing a rebellious, unbelieving generation that rejects the truth. Jesus Himself said, *"A wicked and adulterous generation seeks after a sign"* (Matthew 12:39).

We Wrestle not...

This is not a "devil issue" but a priority issue, a warning about valuing signs above truth. The problem is not demons masquerading as gifts; it is people forsaking the Word in pursuit of manifestations. The solution is not suspicion, but Scripture.

False Prophets – Human Deceivers, Not Demonic Possession

"Beware of false prophets... You will know them by their fruits." — **Matthew 7:15–16, NKJV**

False prophets are not necessarily vessels of demons. They are deceivers, self-promoting, manipulative people who operate from selfish ambition. The problem here is intentional deception by people, not demonic takeover of sincere believers. Jesus said we would know them by their fruits, not by their manifestations. Discerning character, not chasing demons, is the biblical model.

Gifts and Callings Are Without Repentance

"Many will say to Me in that day, 'Lord, Lord, have we not prophesied... cast out demons... done many wonders in Your name?'" — **Matthew 7:22–23, NKJV**

Jesus is not exposing demonic infiltration here. He is revealing that illegitimate ministry can still produce supernatural results. The gifts and callings of God are irrevocable (Romans 11:29). The issue is not the gift, but the heart. These people were lawless, not because of what they operated in, but because they never knew Him. This is not about deception through spirits; it's about doing ministry without legitimacy or authorization.

The Slave Girl in Acts 16 – A Case of Deliverance, Not Dualism

"This girl followed Paul... saying, 'These men are the servants of the Most High God.'" — **Acts 16:17, NKJV**

The girl had a legitimate spiritual problem, and Paul exercised apostolic authority to deal with it. This was not a lesson in identifying subtle deceptions in prophetic speech, nor a reason to fear imitation in the gifts of the Spirit. It was a clear demonic oppression that needed deliverance, and it was dealt with. No mapping. No months of discernment. No fear. No "wrestling".

Furthermore, Paul naturally discerned, he wasn't vulnerable to being deceived by this spirit. Like all believers He was sealed by the Spirit and awakened to the voice of the Spirit within him.

Sealed, Not Suspicious

The danger of spiritual warfare teaching is not just in what it says, but in what it implies: that the blood of Jesus was not enough, that the believer must constantly question whether what they hear, feel, or sense might be the devil in disguise.

But the truth is this:

"You were sealed with the Holy Spirit of promise." — **Ephesians 1:13, NKJV**

"The anointing... teaches you concerning all things, and is true, and is not a lie." — **1 John 2:27, NKJV**

We do not live in fear of deception. We live in the discernment of sonship. We are not constantly scanning for spiritual contaminants; we are overflowing with rivers of living water.

Watchman Nee's desire was sincere. But the theology that followed was not sovereign. It turned discernment into suspicion, and gifts into potential gateways for darkness. Let us not guard against the Holy Spirit. Let us yield to Him. Let us not fear the devil's imitation, let us abide in Christ's revelation.

Agnes Sanford (1897–1982)

Agnes Sanford is widely recognized as a pioneer of the inner healing movement, but her emphasis was not on the demonic, it was overwhelmingly on freedom through forgiveness, emotional healing, and the power of the Holy Spirit to restore the inner life.

Core Emphases of Agnes Sanford's Inner Healing Ministry:

Healing Through Forgiveness
- Sanford taught that unforgiveness and emotional wounds could become blockages to spiritual and physical health.
- She emphasized forgiving others, receiving God's forgiveness, and self-forgiveness as essential components of healing.
- Her model invited the Holy Spirit into painful memories so that healing could occur in the heart, mind, and emotions, not by analyzing trauma but by receiving divine love.

We Wrestle not...

Prayer and the Presence of Christ
- She believed in inviting Christ into the memory or wound, not to cast out demons, but to bring healing to a specific moment in a person's life.
- This is sometimes referred to as "healing of the memories."
- Sanford was deeply Christ-centered and prayer-focused, rather than warfare-oriented.

Spiritual Dynamics, but Not Fear-Based
- While she acknowledged the existence of evil and spiritual influence, she did not center her ministry on demonic manifestations.
- She believed most emotional and spiritual pain came from broken relationships, trauma, and woundedness, not necessarily demonization.
- Her writings promote a peaceful, gentle approach to healing, very different from the aggressive, confrontational model seen in later spiritual warfare movements.

The Creative Power of God's Love
- Sanford viewed God's power as creative and restorative, not primarily combative.
- She compared prayer to a flow of divine energy that must be received and released by faith, in alignment with God's love.

In Her Own Words

From *'The Healing Light'* (one of her most influential books):

"We must forgive not only with the head, but with the heart. The act of forgiveness must be followed by a feeling of love and peace... it is then that healing can truly begin."

Agnes Sanford's emphasis was not the demonic, but divine healing through love, forgiveness, and the presence of Christ. She laid the groundwork for what would later be termed "inner healing," but her theology was far more pastoral than confrontational.

While later ministries may have attached deliverance models to her ideas, Sanford herself was not a spiritual warfare teacher in the modern sense. She offered a gentle, Spirit-led approach to restoring the soul, grounded in grace, not fear.

Contemporary influences: Strategic warfare takes the stage

The late 20th century witnessed a complete shift. No longer were Christians called to resist temptation and grow in Christ. Now, the focus became confronting demons, in the air, over cities, in governments, even in geographical regions.

C. Peter Wagner (1930–2016) and the Doctrine of Spiritual Warfare

C. Peter Wagner was a leading voice in the modern spiritual warfare movement, particularly through his leadership in the New Apostolic Reformation (NAR). Wagner's teachings dramatically influenced the Church's understanding of spiritual warfare, introducing concepts like strategic-level warfare, territorial spirits, spiritual mapping, and apostolic dominion. This section examines Wagner's major claims and offers Kingdom-based counterpoints that realign spiritual warfare with the finished work of Christ.

Strategic-Level Spiritual Warfare

Wagner taught that certain high-ranking demons (principalities) rule over regions, cities, and nations, and must be directly confronted through united prayer efforts led by apostolic leaders.

Kingdom Counterpoint:

Ephesians 6:12 acknowledges spiritual principalities, but Colossians 2:15 clearly states they have been disarmed. The early Church never targeted spirits over cities, they preached the Gospel and trusted Christ's reign. Authority is exercised through discipleship, not confrontation.

Spiritual Mapping

Wagner promoted researching the history and strongholds of specific cities or regions to discern the spiritual dynamics and identify demons responsible for darkness in those areas.

Kingdom Counterpoint:

Jesus never instructed His followers to investigate demons. Paul never engaged in spiritual mapping. Instead, the Church is called to proclaim light, not study darkness (2 Cor. 4:5–6). Spiritual climates change when truth is preached, not when demons are traced.

We Wrestle not...

Territorial Spirits Must Be Bound to Advance the Gospel

Wagner asserted that territorial spirits block evangelism and must be bound or cast down before effective ministry can occur in a region.

Kingdom Counterpoint:

This concept contradicts Acts 8, where Philip preached in Samaria and the city was filled with joy, no mention of binding spirits. Jesus said, 'I will build My Church, and the gates of hell shall not prevail against it' (Matt. 16:18). No spiritual reconnaissance is needed, just the Gospel.

Apostolic Intercession and Warfare

Wagner believed only recognized apostles had the authority to wage high-level warfare and lead intercessory efforts over cities and nations.

Kingdom Counterpoint:

All believers are seated with Christ (Eph. 2:6). The 'effectual fervent prayer' of the righteous avails much (James 5:16). Jesus is the only Mediator (1 Tim. 2:5). The idea of elite warfare leaders creates hierarchy where Christ has created equality among His body.

Revival Requires Breaking Spiritual Resistance in the Heavenlies

Wagner taught that revival is delayed by strongholds in the heavens that need to be torn down through spiritual warfare.

Kingdom Counterpoint:

Revival comes through repentance and the Word of God. Nowhere in Scripture is revival linked to heavenly combat. The early Church saw revival through preaching, unity, and the power of the Holy Spirit, not by engaging invisible forces.

Conclusion: Reclaiming a Kingdom Lens

C. Peter Wagner's teachings gave language and structure to a movement that placed too much emphasis on darkness and too little on the finished work of Jesus Christ. His doctrine elevated human strategy over divine simplicity. The Kingdom perspective offers rest instead of striving, light instead of fear, and sonship instead of spiritual elitism. True warfare is not reclaiming land from devils, it is reclaiming minds with truth. Let the Church return to Christ-centered proclamation, and the darkness will flee.

References and Source Acknowledgments

C. Peter Wagner, *Confronting the Powers: How the New Testament Church Experienced the Power of Strategic-Level Spiritual Warfare* (Regal Books, 1996).
C. Peter Wagner, *Engaging the Enemy: How to Fight and Defeat Territorial Spirits* (Regal Books, 1991).
C. Peter Wagner, *Prayer Shield: How to Intercede for Pastors, Christian Leaders and Others on the Spiritual Frontlines* (Regal Books, 1992).
C. Peter Wagner, *Dominion!: How Kingdom Action Can Change the World* (Chosen Books, 2008).
For further critique and analysis, see: Chuck Lowe, *Territorial Spirits and World Evangelization?* (Mentor/Christian Focus, 1998).

There are many others that have influenced the church in spiritual warfare. The close examination of their ideas measured against the early church fathers, scripture, and the function of the New Testament church, makes clear the cracks in the foundation of this doctrine.

I am persuaded, that the modern era of warfare engagement is rooted in the utmost sincerity to protect, warn, and guide the church. Often times, when falsities are overlayed with sincerity, they are acceptable because of the motive in which they originated. Sincerity must never transcend truth.

Conclusion: Return to the Kingdom

The journey from New Testament apostolic proclamation to modern warfare doctrine is not one of enlightenment but of erosion. The further the Church drifts from Christ's finished work, the more we are tempted to fight rather than stand.

We Wrestle not...

Modern spiritual warfare often resembles a paranoid campaign rather than a triumphant Kingdom life.

"For we wrestle not..." does not mean we engage in endless conflict, it means we recognize where our fight lies: not with devils, but with doubt; not in the air, but in the mind; not for victory, but from it.

It is time for the Church to reclaim the Gospel of the Kingdom, rooted in identity, authority, rest, and victory. The Son of God has triumphed. The true warfare is to believe it.

The general notion is that spiritual warfare is mostly a Christian construct. Wikipedia defines spiritual warfare as the Christian concept of fighting against the work of preternatural evil forces.

The Language of Conflict: When Terms Collide

Part of the confusion in modern theology stems from the phrase itself: spiritual warfare. These two words, when rightly defined, each hold weight and clarity in Scripture.

- *Spiritual* refers to that which is of the Spirit, invisible but eternal, divine in origin or demonic in distortion.
- *Warfare* speaks to conflict, struggle, or confrontation.

But when these words are joined without precision, they often become a breeding ground for theological dualism, the idea that light and darkness are in equal opposition, locked in an eternal struggle for dominance. This is not the Gospel. God has no rival.

We Wrestle not...

"I am the Lord, and there is no other; There is no God besides Me." — **Isaiah 45:5, NKJV**

"I am God, and there is no other; I am God, and there is none like Me." — **Isaiah 46:9, NKJV**

"Before Me there was no God formed, Nor shall there be after Me." — **Isaiah 43:10, NKJV**

Christ has already conquered. The Holy Spirit does not wrestle with demons; He displaces them.

"Spiritual warfare" as a term has, in many circles, collapsed into a catch-all that justifies fear, fosters superstition, and shifts focus away from Christ's finished work. It too easily becomes an excuse for ongoing struggle rather than an invitation to rest, reign, and renew the mind.

When believers adopt this undefined, hybrid language, they unintentionally conflate the internal conflict of belief with external enemies of flesh and blood. They blur the line between resisting temptation and battling geography. And they forget that Christ is seated, not striving, and we are seated with Him.

We Wrestle not...

Reflection prompt:

1. When you hear the term spiritual warfare, what images or emotions immediately come to mind? Are they rooted in Scripture or cultural teaching?
2. How have you seen the Church shift from standing in victory to striving for it?
3. In what ways can your understanding of warfare be redefined by Christ's triumph and your seated identity in Him?
4. Do you find yourself more focused on fighting the enemy or growing in sonship? What does that reveal?
5. How might reclaiming a Kingdom lens change the way you pray, preach, or disciple others regarding conflict and victory?

CHAPTER SEVEN
THE DEVIL'S SPOTLIGHT

Exposing the Imbalance of Demon-Centric Theology

Introduction

Modern spiritual warfare literature often reads more like a demonic encyclopedia than a declaration of Christ's victory. Books like Howard Pittman's *'Demons, Demons, Demons'*, Rebecca Brown's *'He Came to Set the Captives Free'*, and C. Peter Wagner's writings on strategic-level warfare have saturated Christian thought with a focus on Satanic hierarchy, deliverance rituals, and supernatural paranoia.

This chapter examines the roots, flaws, and consequences of this theology, and presents the Gospel of the Kingdom as the corrective lens.

The Common Themes in Demon-Focused Theology

Many modern books portray Satan's power as overwhelming, almost omnipresent. Common themes include:

- Territorial spirits ruling over regions
- Constant need for deliverance from demons
- Believers unknowingly under demonic influence
- Strategic warfare tactics to "break through" spiritual darkness

We Wrestle not…

While these perspectives are dramatic, they often do more to exalt Satan's power than Christ's finished work.

Underlying Assumptions and Their Errors

Satan controls the atmosphere and regions.
Kingdom Counterpoint: *"All authority has been given to Me in heaven and on earth"* (Matt. 28:18). Jesus reigns now.

Believers must fight constantly for their freedom.
Kingdom Counterpoint: *"He has delivered us from the power of darkness"* (Col. 1:13). The fight is to believe, not to battle.

The Church must identify and bind territorial spirits.
Kingdom Counterpoint: The apostles never practiced or taught this. They simply preached Christ, planted churches, and transformed culture through truth.

Spiritual manifestations must be scrutinized for demonic imitation.
Kingdom Counterpoint: *"You are complete in Him"* (Col. 2:10). The Holy Spirit doesn't operate in fear or confusion.

We Wrestle not...

Modern Spiritual Warfare vs. Kingdom Reality

Modern View	Kingdom Reality
Satan controls systems	"The earth is the Lord's" (Ps. 24:1)
Demons behind every problem	"You are complete in Him" (Col. 2:10)
Constant need for deliverance	"He has delivered us from the power of darkness" (Col. 1:13)
Territorial spirits rule cities	"Ask of Me, and I will give You the nations" (Ps. 2:8)
Prayer must 'break through'	"Let us come boldly to the throne of grace" (Heb. 4:16)

The Result: Fear, Not Faith

Christians shaped by demon-centric theology often live exhausted, hyper-vigilant lives. Their worldview is built on suspicion. Instead of resting in sonship, they remain in survival mode, afraid of dreams, thoughts, or emotional responses that might indicate demonic presence. But the Kingdom invites us to live from peace, not paranoia.

Restoring the Kingdom Focus

The early Church knew of demons, but they were not obsessed with them. Their emphasis was on the reign of Jesus, the transformation of hearts, and the advancing of the Kingdom. The greatest threat to darkness was not warfare prayers, it was the Gospel.

We Wrestle not...

Let us once again place the spotlight on the King. Let the doctrine of demons be replaced by the doctrine of Christ. Let the saints rest in the finished work of the cross, and declare the victory already won.

Kingdom Counterpoints to Demon-Centric Teachings

Many popular books have influenced the modern Church's understanding of spiritual warfare, often emphasizing demonic engagement over Gospel-centered truth. This section presents direct doctrinal quotes or summaries from key works and provides Kingdom-based counterpoints rooted in Scripture and Christ's finished work.

'Pigs in the Parlor' – Frank Hammond

Quote: *"Every Christian needs deliverance, and many need it often. The Christian must be aggressive in seeking freedom from demons."*

Kingdom Counterpoint:

Colossians 1:13 (NKJV) – *"He has delivered us from the power of darkness and conveyed us into the kingdom of the Son of His love."*

Deliverance is not a cycle of defeat; it is a finished transaction. The believer's posture is one of freedom and maturity, not dependency on deliverance rituals.

We Wrestle not…

What does it mean to be a Christian relative to freedom from demons?

To be a Christian means to be in Christ, joined to Him by faith, sealed with the Holy Spirit, and no longer under the dominion of darkness.

"Therefore, if anyone is in Christ, he is a new creation…"
— **2 Corinthians 5:17, NKJV**

Being in Christ is not partial ownership, it's total transformation. You are not dual owned. You are God's possession (1 Peter 2:9). Deliverance is not something Christians must constantly seek, it is something we walk out by truth and transformation, not by ongoing rituals.

Are we not free from demons when we are surrendered to Christ?

Yes. Freedom is not something we achieve; it is something we receive. When we surrender to Christ, we are no longer under Satan's dominion.

"If the Son makes you free, you shall be free indeed." — **John 8:36, NKJV**

"Stand fast therefore in the liberty by which Christ has made us free…" — **Galatians 5:1, NKJV**

While we do renew our minds (Romans 12:2), that is a process of growing in truth and maturity, not a deliverance from indwelling demons. The Holy Spirit does not cohabitate with unclean spirits.

We Wrestle not…

Can we be "owned" by both God and the devil?

Absolutely not.

"You were bought at a price; do not become slaves of men."
— **1 Corinthians 7:23, NKJV**

"No one can serve two masters…" — **Matthew 6:24, NKJV**

When Jesus redeemed you by His blood, He didn't lease you, He purchased you fully. To say a believer can be "owned" or "inhabited" by a demon is to undermine the power of redemption and the sufficiency of Christ's atonement.

Was the blood not a sufficient price?

The blood of Jesus was not only sufficient, but it was also final and eternal.

"With His own blood He entered the Most Holy Place once for all, having obtained eternal redemption." — **Hebrews 9:12, NKJV**

"You are not your own… for you were bought at a price."
— **1 Corinthians 6:19–20, NKJV**

To teach that Christians must continually seek deliverance from demons is to diminish the cross and place more confidence in the devil's ability to harass than in Christ's ability to keep.

You were bought, sealed, rescued, and joined to Christ. No demon can claim you. No spirit can co-occupy you. You don't need to fight for freedom, you need to believe and walk in it.

We Wrestle not...

The false teaching that "every Christian needs deliverance, and many need it often" contradicts the heart of the Gospel. The early Church called believers saints, not hosts of demons. Your body is a temple of the Holy Spirit, not a timeshare with unclean spirits.

'He Came to Set the Captives Free' – Rebecca Brown

Quote: *"Christians can have demons and need to constantly fight Satan's attempts to infiltrate their lives."*

Kingdom Counterpoint:

2 Corinthians 5:17 (NKJV) – *"Therefore, if anyone is in Christ, he is a new creation; old things have passed away; behold, all things have become new."*

A Kingdom Response to Demon Possession Theology

This statement strikes at the very heart of the Gospel. It implies that a person can be both redeemed and owned, both a son and a slave, both filled with the Spirit and inhabited by demons. This is not only biblically inaccurate, it is spiritually harmful, eroding the confidence of believers in the blood of Christ and exalting the presence of the enemy over the power of God.

The Cross Does Not Lease, It Redeems

"In Him we have redemption through His blood, the forgiveness of sins, according to the riches of His grace." — **Ephesians 1:7, NKJV**

We Wrestle not...

Redemption is not partial. It's not ongoing in terms of possession. The word redeem means to purchase back, to transfer ownership legally and fully. To say that a believer can "have demons" after redemption is to say that Christ's blood wasn't enough to complete the transfer.

Sons Are Not Co-Owned

"But as many as received Him, to them He gave the right [exousia] to become children of God, to those who believe in His name." — **John 1:12, NKJV**

The word exousia means legal authority or right. When a believer receives Christ, they are given the legal standing of sonship, a place of inheritance, ownership, and divine identity. You cannot simultaneously be a son of God and possessed by Satan. That is spiritual doublemindedness.

The Spirit and Demons Do Not Co-Dwell

"What communion has light with darkness? ... Or what agreement has the temple of God with idols?" — **2 Corinthians 6:14–16, NKJV**

Believers are temples of the Holy Spirit (1 Cor. 6:19). The idea that a temple filled with God's Spirit can also be occupied by demons is a contradiction in terms. Light and darkness cannot share space.

Confidence in Christ, Not Continual Suspicion of Satan

Demon-centric doctrines like Brown's create fear-based faith, constantly monitoring emotions, thoughts, and behaviors as possible demonic infiltration. This undermines

We Wrestle not...

the New Testament model of rest, sonship, and maturity in Christ.

"You are complete in Him, who is the head of all principality and power." — **Colossians 2:10, NKJV**

We are not incomplete Christians still battling for ownership. We are complete, sealed, and seated with Christ (Eph. 2:6). Our warfare is not to reclaim ownership, it is to stand in the ownership already secured.

The doctrine that Christians can "have demons" is incompatible with the Gospel. It turns saints into suspects. It dishonors the blood of Christ. And it diminishes the legal authority of redemption. The finished work of Christ did not fail to evict Satan, it triumphed over him.

"Having disarmed principalities and powers, He made a public spectacle of them, triumphing over them in it." — **Colossians 2:15, NKJV**

'The Bondage Breaker' *– Neil T. Anderson*

Quote*:* *"To be free, you must renounce Satan's lies, go through a detailed inventory of sins, and break strongholds by confession and declaration."*

Kingdom Counterpoint:

John 8:32 (NKJV) – *"And you shall know the truth, and the truth shall make you free."*

We Wrestle not...

Debunking Performance-Based Deliverance: A Kingdom Response

This quote teaches a formulaic and introspective path to freedom, one that emphasizes human effort, exhaustive confession, and mental self-cleansing as the means of deliverance. While confession has a biblical place, this model turns freedom into a performance, shifting the believer's focus from Christ's sufficiency to their own introspection.

Strongholds Are Not Personal Sins Listed, They Are Mindsets Opposing Truth

"For the weapons of our warfare are not carnal but mighty in God for pulling down strongholds, casting down arguments and every high thing that exalts itself against the knowledge of God..." — **2 Corinthians 10:4–5 (NKJV)**

Paul defines strongholds not as unconfessed sins but as thought patterns, belief systems, and philosophies that oppose the knowledge of God. The way to break strongholds is not through confession of every past act, but through the apostolic proclamation of truth that dismantles lies.

The Heart Is Not Fully Known by Man

"The heart is deceitful above all things, and desperately wicked; who can know it?" — **Jeremiah 17:9 (NKJV)**

If freedom depended on us remembering and renouncing every sin, it would never be achieved. The Gospel does not require perfect recall. It calls for perfect surrender to the finished work of Christ.

We Wrestle not...

Truth, Not Inventory, Sets Us Free

"And you shall know the truth, and the truth shall make you free." — **John 8:32 (NKJV)**

Jesus didn't say freedom comes from a step-by-step inventory. He said it comes from truth. Apostolic teaching, Gospel-centered preaching, and Spirit-led discipleship pull down strongholds, not religious checklists.

Confession Is Not the Pathway to Deliverance, Faith Is

"Therefore, having been justified by faith, we have peace with God through our Lord Jesus Christ..." — **Romans 5:1 (NKJV)**

Confession has value in repentance and accountability, but it does not earn deliverance. Freedom was purchased at the cross and accessed by faith, not formula.

Apostolic Strategy Pulls Down Strongholds

In Acts, Paul didn't take people through inventories of sins. He preached Christ, reasoned from Scripture, and taught Kingdom truth. The early Church's "stronghold breaking" was done through apostolic teaching and discipleship, not spiritual inventory checklists.

The quote from *'The Bondage Breaker'* distorts the Gospel by making freedom conditional on personal performance. It burdens believers with a checklist mentality instead of inviting them into restful, confident faith in the finished work of Christ. The Kingdom path to freedom is truth proclaimed, believed, and walked in, not stronghold-by-stronghold self-analysis.

We Wrestle not...

'Prayers That Rout Demons' – John Eckhardt

Quote: *"We must speak aggressively against spirits to take back what the enemy has stolen. Spiritual warfare requires violent prayer and declarations."*

Kingdom Counterpoint:

Ephesians 6:13 (NKJV) – *"Therefore take up the whole armor of God, that you may be able to withstand in the evil day, and having done all, to stand."*

What Is the Biblical Premise for Speaking Aggressively Against Spirits?

There is no biblical command or example of believers being told to speak aggressively to demons in prayer. The only people who directly addressed demons in Scripture were:

- Jesus, as the Son of God with full authority
- The Apostles, when casting out demons, not during prayer

In fact, when we're given insight into a spiritual confrontation, even an angel does not act presumptuously:

"Yet Michael the archangel, in contending with the devil… dared not bring against him a reviling accusation, but said, 'The Lord rebuke you!'" — **Jude 1:9, NKJV**

If Michael the archangel refused to confront Satan directly with accusations, what gives believers the idea that we should command, insult, or battle demons in prayer?

We Wrestle not...

What Is "Violent Prayer"?

This is a charismatic invention, not a biblical term. It's often justified using Matthew 11:12:

"The kingdom of heaven suffers violence, and the violent take it by force." — **Matthew 11:12, NKJV**

Many interpret this to mean:
- "Prayer must be aggressive."
- "Spiritual warfare requires violent shouting."
- "We have to violently bind devils and tear down strongholds."

This has led to the popular but unbiblical phrase: "violent prayers get violent results."

But that's not what Jesus meant.

The Kingdom Is Forcefully Advancing

The verse describes how:
- The Kingdom of God is breaking into the world with such power and urgency that it stirs radical, even disruptive, responses.
- Those who respond to it, like John the Baptist's followers and Jesus' early disciples, are seizing it with conviction, pressing into it boldly, often at great cost.

The Greek word translated "violent" (biazō) means:
- "to press into with intensity,"
- "to forcefully advance,"
- not "to act with aggression against spirits."

We Wrestle not…

Other Translations Clarify This:
- ESV:

"*The kingdom of heaven has suffered violence, and the violent take it by force.*"

- NLT:

"*The Kingdom of Heaven has been forcefully advancing, and violent people are attacking it.*"

- Amplified:

"*The kingdom of heaven has endured violent assault, and violent men seize it by force [as a precious prize—a share in the heavenly kingdom is sought with most ardent zeal and intense exertion].*"

Kingdom Context:

- Jesus is describing how the arrival of the Kingdom is so disruptive and transformational that people are pressing into it with zeal, even at the cost of persecution, imprisonment (John), and martyrdom.
- This is not about the volume of our prayers, but the urgency of our surrender and the unapologetic faith with which we pursue the Kingdom.

"Violent prayer" is not a biblical concept.

Matthew 11:12 refers to the radical response to the breaking-in of the Kingdom, not to shouting at demons.

Biblical prayer is:
- Addressed to God the Father (Matthew 6:9)
- In the name of Jesus (John 14:13)
- Empowered by the Holy Spirit (Romans 8:26)

We Wrestle not...

It is never directed at Satan.

Are We Praying to Demons?

When someone says in prayer, "Satan, I bind you," or "Devil, you cannot do this," they are in essence addressing the devil. That is not prayer, it is conversation or confrontation with a spirit.

Prayer is to God alone.

"Our Father in heaven, hallowed be Your name..." — *Matthew 6:9, NKJV*

To "pray" to a demon, even if it's rebuking, commanding, or binding, is a misuse of prayer and a dangerous shift in spiritual posture. It opens believers to deception by focusing their spiritual energy on the enemy instead of on the supremacy of Christ.

How Are Violent Prayers Against Demons Expressed?

In books like Prayers That Rout Demons, violent prayers are expressed as:
- Shouting, commanding, and aggressively naming spirits
- Using spiritual language to "pull down," "crush," or "destroy" enemies
- Speaking in warfare tones often aimed more at the enemy than toward God

This is nowhere found in the New Testament model of prayer. Paul prayed for wisdom, revelation, strength in the inner man, and boldness to preach, not to defeat devils through violent declarations.

The Apostolic Model: Victory by Standing, Not Shouting

"Put on the whole armor of God... and having done all, to stand." — **Ephesians 6:11, 13, NKJV**

"Resist him, steadfast in the faith..." — **1 Peter 5:9, NKJV**

Paul never told believers to speak to the devil. He told them to stand, resist, and walk in truth. The enemy is defeated not by our aggressive tone, but by our firm stance in faith and truth, and consistent faith filled living.

The Church must return to Christ-centered prayer, not demon-directed declarations. The aggression of modern warfare language reflects fear, not faith.

It sounds bold but it distracts from the authority of the King who already triumphed.

"Let us therefore come boldly to the throne of grace..." — **Hebrews 4:16**

Let's pray to the Father, stand in the Son, and trust the Spirit, and let the devil flee as truth is lived out.

Derek Prince Writings – General

Quote: *"Many problems—sickness, depression, poverty—are caused by demons and must be cast out for healing to occur."*

Kingdom Counterpoint:

Romans 8:2 (NKJV) – *"For the law of the Spirit of life in Christ Jesus has made me free from the law of sin and death."*

Kingdom Response: Are Sickness, Depression, and Poverty Caused by Demons?

Biblical Acknowledgment of Demonic Influence

Scripture does show that some physical or mental afflictions have demonic origins. Jesus cast out spirits that caused muteness (Mark 9:25), seizures (Matthew 17:14–18), and a 'spirit of infirmity' (Luke 13:11–13). However, not all sickness or suffering is attributed to demons in Scripture, and the New Testament epistles do not instruct believers to treat such conditions as demonic by default.

The Role of the Fall: 'In the Day You Eat... You Shall Die'

Genesis 2:17 marks the origin of human suffering through Adam's disobedience. This opened the door to spiritual death, physical decay, toil, shame, and brokenness. Romans 5:12 confirms that death and suffering spread to all humanity through sin. Thus, many struggles today—sickness, depression, poverty—are often consequences of the fallen world, not direct demonic attack.

We Wrestle not…

Human and Natural Origins of Sickness, Poverty, and Depression

Sickness is often due to lifestyle, diet, or genetics. Poverty may stem from poor financial management, systemic injustice, or laziness (Proverbs 6:10–11). Depression can result from trauma, chemical imbalances, or distorted thinking. Scripture calls for wisdom, stewardship, healing, and the renewal of the mind (Romans 12:2) rather than defaulting to deliverance for every condition.

Discernment, Not Assumption

1 John 4:1 reminds believers to 'test the spirits.' Paul gave instruction to the Church on healing (James 5:14), managing anxiety (Philippians 4:6–8), and walking in spiritual authority, none of which included automatic exorcism. The Church must avoid reducing every struggle to demonic possession. Deliverance is one tool, not the entire toolbox of Kingdom life.

While some sickness, torment, and bondage may be demonic in origin, not all struggles are caused by demons. Many result from living in a fallen world, human choices, or natural consequences. The solution is not always deliverance, it is wisdom, healing, stewardship, and discipleship in the truth. Christ came not only to cast out devils but to renew the mind, heal the heart, and restore the soul.

The voices of demons may be loud in today's theology, but the King is still seated. His reign is not threatened. His blood is not challenged. And His Church is not prey, we are priests, kings, and sons. Let us unseat the doctrines of fear and restore the Gospel of the Kingdom.

We Wrestle not...

Reflection Prompts

1. According to Scripture, who should be the primary focus of our prayers, God or the devil?
2. Compare the model of spiritual warfare seen in the lives of Jesus and Paul with the teachings found in modern books like Pigs in the Parlor or Prayers That Rout Demons.
3. Are there any areas where you have been taught to fear the devil more than trust in the finished work of Christ?
4. What is the danger of turning every issue, sickness, poverty, depression, into a demonic problem?
5. Evaluate this quote: "To be free, you must go through a detailed inventory of sins and renounce Satan's lies." What's the difference between faith-based freedom and performance-based deliverance?
6. Jesus said, "It is finished." What does this mean to you in the context of spiritual warfare?

CHAPTER EIGHT
THE CURSE STOPS HERE

One of the most persistent teachings in modern spiritual warfare circles is the concept of generational curses, the belief that the sins, failures, and demonic assignments of our forefathers pass down through the bloodline, wreaking havoc in the lives of believers unless aggressively broken through special prayers, confessions, or rituals.

This concept, while rooted in portions of the Old Covenant, fails to understand the greater truth of the New Creation in Christ. It keeps believers tethered to an identity that died with Christ and resurrected into something altogether new. It assumes that what God has declared blessed can be overwritten by a curse.

The Old Covenant Framework

The origin of generational curse doctrine finds grounding in texts such as Exodus 20:5, where God says He visits *"the iniquity of the fathers upon the children unto the third and fourth generation of them that hate me."* Under the Old Covenant, when the law governed relationship and judgment, this consequence was real. Covenant-breaking invited calamity, often affecting descendants. However, this was a covenant of types and shadows, pointing to the need for a greater redemption.

By the time we reach the prophet Ezekiel, God is already shifting the narrative: *"The soul that sins shall die. The son shall not bear the iniquity of the father"* (Ezekiel 18:20). He was preparing Israel for a day when personal responsibility would surpass generational identity.

The Curse Met the Cross

Everything changed at the cross.

"Cursed is every man who hangs upon a tree" (Galatians 3:13, quoting Deuteronomy 21:23).

Paul declares that Christ became a curse for us so that the blessing of Abraham might come upon the Gentiles. In this single, cosmic exchange, every inherited curse was absorbed by the spotless Lamb.

Balaam, a pagan prophet, unknowingly prophesied an eternal truth when he said, *"I cannot curse what God has blessed"* (Numbers 23:8).

The blood of Jesus permanently blessed those who are in Christ, before their earthly birth and even before the foundation of the world (Ephesians 1:3–5). God did not bless us on the condition of earthly lineage, but according to His eternal purpose.

If God declared us blessed, who can reverse it? No demonic strategy, ancestral sin, or cultural superstition can override the blessing encoded into our identity in Christ.

A New Genealogy

The fundamental flaw in generational curse doctrine is the assumption that our spiritual identity is tied to our natural genealogy. It is not. Jesus made it clear in John 3: *"You must be born again."*

That rebirth reassigns our origin.

We no longer come from our earthly parents; we came through them. We come from God. He is now our Father.

"If any man be in Christ, he is a new creation" (2 Corinthians 5:17). Not a cleaned-up version of the old, not a cursed man trying to break free. He is new. Old things: curses, patterns, dysfunctions, are passed away. All things are made new.

To continue identifying with generational curses is to deny the power of our new birth and undermine the sufficiency of the cross.

The Bloodline of the Redeemed

The blood of Jesus doesn't just wash sin, it rewrites DNA. It doesn't only redeem behavior, it reclaims bloodlines. Jesus is the last Adam, and we are no longer tied to the lineage of the first Adam. We have been grafted into a divine genealogy.

Hebrews 7:3 describes Melchizedek as "without genealogy," foreshadowing a priesthood that would not rely on natural descent. Jesus, after the order of Melchizedek, inaugurates a spiritual priesthood born not of blood, nor of the will of the flesh, but of God (John 1:13).

We Wrestle not...

The Real Warfare: Renewing the Mind

The battle isn't in breaking off generational curses, it's in renewing the mind to believe what God has already done. As Paul said, *"Be transformed by the renewing of your mind"* (Romans 12:2), not the rewriting of your past.

Warfare is not shouting down curses that Christ already absorbed. It's standing confidently in the identity you received through Him. Instead of teaching believers to diagnose bloodlines, Scripture teaches them to walk in truth.

Integrity: The True Generational Breakthrough

While some focus on prayers to break family curses, scripture offers a different strategy for generational blessing:

"The righteous man walks in his integrity; his children are blessed after him" **(Proverbs 20:7, NKJV).**

This isn't a mystical ritual, it's a principal promise. A man of integrity doesn't have to spend his life rebuking spirits or renouncing curses over his children. His walk breaks the cycle. His character becomes the intercessor.

God honors the life of a man who walks uprightly. Integrity becomes a seed, and the harvest is generational blessing. The father's righteous decisions build a foundation for his children's destiny.

This is not generational cursing; it is generational building.

We Wrestle not...

Jesus Did Not Cast Out Generational Curses

Jesus never addressed or broke generational curses in His ministry. People were healed or delivered by faith. If curses were an issue in the New Covenant, He would have dealt with them.

Jesus Traced to David, Not to Adam's Fall

Jesus' genealogy in Matthew connects Him to David and Abraham, not to Adam's failure. Luke's genealogy shows Him as the last Adam, beginning a new lineage.

Colossians 1:13 – We've Changed Kingdoms

We've been transferred from the domain of darkness into the Kingdom of the Son. Generational curses belong to the old domain.

Christ is the Firstborn Among Many Brethren

Romans 8:29 calls Jesus the firstborn among many. If He is our brother, we are in a new family, no longer cursed but blessed.

Blessing Came Before the Law (Abrahamic Blessing)

Galatians 3 proves the blessing of Abraham predates the law. Curses came with the law, but inheritance came by promise.

Ephesians 2 – One New Man

Christ abolished distinctions and created one new man. This new creation is not tied to generational identities.

We Wrestle not…

Hebrews 8 – A Better Covenant with Better Promises

We are under a new covenant, unlike the one made with the fathers. This one carries no curses, only righteousness and inheritance.

1 Peter 1:18–19 – Redeemed from Vain Inheritance

We were redeemed from the vain traditions of our fathers with the precious blood of Christ. No inherited bondage remains.

Isaiah 53 – He Bore Our Iniquities

Jesus bore the iniquity of us all, including ancestral iniquity. We are no longer carriers of generational dysfunction.

Closing Declaration

In Christ, the curse is broken. My identity is not found in my bloodline but in the blood of Jesus. I have been made new. I am not cursed; I am blessed with every spiritual blessing in heavenly places. I walk in integrity, and my children are blessed after me. No past can override the promise. The curse stops here, in Jesus' name.

We Wrestle not…

Reflection Prompts

1. What does it mean to come through your parents but not from them?
2. How does integrity create generational blessing according to Proverbs 20:7?
3. Why is the doctrine of generational curses incompatible with the new creation in Christ?
4. What areas of your mindset need to be renewed to align with your identity in Christ?

CHAPTER NINE
Strategic-Level Warfare

"Let us therefore be diligent to enter that rest, lest anyone fall after the same example of disobedience."
— **Hebrews 4:11, NKJV**

Much of what is taught today under the banner of spiritual warfare is well-meaning yet misaligned with the finished work of Christ. Many modern doctrines, particularly those popularized by figures such as previously mentioned, have drawn the Church into a restless battle posture, often leaving believers weary, striving, and distracted.

This chapter is not written to shame these teachers or those who have followed them. Rather, it is a call to clarity, a gracious correction to redirect God's people back to rest, authority, and truth. We are not called to conquer darkness, but to walk in the light. We are not told to fight devils, but to labor to enter rest.

Strategic-level spiritual warfare

C. Peter Wagner's Book: *'Confronting the Powers'*

Wagner argued that early believers engaged in "strategic-level warfare" against demonic powers that ruled over territories and cities. He encouraged believers today to follow suit through corporate intercession, prophetic actions, and spiritual "mapping."

'*In Confronting the Powers: How the New Testament Church Experienced the Power of Strategic-Level Spiritual Warfare*', C. Peter Wagner introduces the concept of "strategic-level spiritual warfare" (SLSW). He defines SLSW as the confrontation of demonic principalities that exert control over geographical regions, distinguishing it from other levels of spiritual warfare. Wagner elaborates on this by stating:

"Strategic-level spiritual warfare incorporates the direct confrontation of territorial spirits, demons believed to be controlling geographical regions in order to dominate people groups."

He further explains that this approach involves practices such as "spiritual mapping," "identificational repentance," and "prophetic acts" to identify and challenge these territorial spirits.

Identificational repentance is a concept popularized by leaders like C. Peter Wagner and others in the New Apostolic Reformation movement. It refers to the act of a person or group repenting on behalf of others, usually their ancestors, nation, city, or ethnic group, for sins they did not personally commit, in hopes of releasing spiritual healing or removing curses from a region.

Key Ideas Behind Identificational Repentance:
- Corporate guilt: The belief that spiritual strongholds or curses can linger over people groups due to past sins (e.g., slavery, idolatry, genocide).
- Spiritual cleansing: By confessing and repenting for those historic sins, modern believers believe they can "cleanse the land" or "break the power" of demonic forces associated with that sin.

We Wrestle not...

- Healing of the land: It is often paired with scriptures like 2 Chronicles 7:14 ("If my people who are called by my name..."), applying them to cities or nations.

Example Practices:
- Confessing national sins like racism, slavery, abortion, or idolatry.
- Public ceremonies with symbolic acts (e.g., pouring out oil, burying declarations).
- Prayer walks, spiritual mapping, and prophetic acts aimed at dislodging "territorial spirits."

Biblical Evaluation:

While corporate intercession is seen in Scripture (e.g., Daniel 9; Nehemiah 1), those acts were often:
- Spirit-led, not formulaic.
- Rooted in covenant relationship, not strategic methods.
- Focused on God's mercy, not demonic territory.

Nowhere does the New Testament teach that we must repent for ancestral sins to break spiritual bondage. In Christ, we are justified by faith and redeemed from the curse (Galatians 3:13). Healing and authority come from Jesus' finished work, not from historical confession ceremonies.

Old Testament Examples of Representative Repentance:

Daniel 9:3–19
Daniel confesses the sins of Israel, including sins he did not personally commit:

We Wrestle not...

"We have sinned and committed iniquity... To the Lord our God belong mercy and forgiveness, though we have rebelled against Him..." (vv. 5, 9)

Daniel stands in intercession for the nation while in exile, based on God's covenant with Israel.

Nehemiah 1:5–7
Nehemiah prays:
"I confess the sins we Israelites, including myself and my father's family, have committed against you."

Ezra 9:6–15
Ezra also confesses generational sins when Israel returns from exile:
"Our sins are higher than our heads and our guilt has reached to the heavens." (v. 6)

Important Observations:

- These were national covenant leaders praying on behalf of Israel, a nation in covenant with God.
- The goal was restoration of covenantal favor, not the spiritual cleansing of geographic regions.
- These prayers came in response to the Law and Prophets, not as spiritual strategies to defeat demons.

New Covenant Contrast:

In the New Testament, no apostle ever calls the Church to repent for ancestral or national sins to gain victory or authority. Rather:
- Each person is accountable for their own sin (Ezekiel 18:20, 2 Corinthians 5:10).

We Wrestle not...

- Jesus bore the sins of the world (John 1:29), and in Him we are redeemed (Galatians 3:13).
- Spiritual victory is not gained through corporate confession, but through faith in Christ's finished work (Colossians 2:13–15).

Identificational repentance, as taught in many modern spiritual warfare movements, would be considered a false or misleading teaching.

PRIESTHOODS: OLD VS. NEW COVENANT

Let's explore the distinctions between the Old Covenant Levitical priesthood and the New Covenant royal priesthood of believers, particularly pertaining to mediation. It also addresses how these truths dismantle the foundations of strategic spiritual warfare and identificational repentance.

Distinctions Between Old and New Priesthoods

Old Covenant Priesthood (Levitical)
- **Tribe:** Levi, sons of Aaron
- **Mediator Role:** Priests stood between God and the people, offering sacrifices for national sin
- **Access:** Only the high priest could enter the Most Holy Place once per year
- **Repetition:** Sacrifices were continual but could not remove sin
- **Orientation:** Ministry was on behalf of men toward God
- **Result:** Temporary cleansing, never complete

New Covenant Royal Priesthood (in Christ)
- **Tribe:** Spiritual (after the order of Melchizedek)

- **Mediator Role:** Christ alone is the Mediator between God and man
- **Access:** All believers have continual access to the Father through Christ
- **Once-for-All:** Jesus offered one perfect sacrifice for all time
- **Orientation:** Ministry is unto God, not on behalf of people
- **Result:** Full atonement and direct access into God's presence

Christ as the Sole Mediator

1 Timothy 2:5 says, *"There is one God and one Mediator between God and men, the Man Christ Jesus."* No believer acts as a mediator for sin. Christ fulfilled that role once for all. Our priesthood is relational and representational, not redemptive.

Strategic Spiritual Warfare: A Misapplied Priesthood

Strategic Level Spiritual Warfare teaches that believers must engage territorial spirits or repent on behalf of regions. This misapplies Old Testament warfare and priestly patterns. Believers are never called to act as mediators for cities or ancestors. The New Testament pattern is truth proclamation and personal transformation, not regional spiritual combat.

Identificational Repentance: A False Priesthood?

Identificational repentance is the act of repenting on behalf of others (e.g., ancestors, nations). This undermines the sufficiency of Christ's atonement and reintroduces a priestly system that Christ fulfilled. The apostolic model focused on preaching, teaching, and praying for revelation, not reenacting Old Covenant rituals.

Our New Priestly Role: Worship, Witness, Word

The New Testament priesthood involves:

- Ministering unto God (Hebrews 13:15; 1 Peter 2:5)
- Declaring His excellencies (1 Peter 2:9)
- Interceding, not to atone, but to align others with the finished work of Christ (Romans 10:1)

We do not break curses or take on roles of national repentance. We minister as sons and priests before God.

Aspect	Old Covenant Priesthood	New Covenant Royal Priesthood
Tribe	Levi	Spiritual (in Christ)
Function	Mediate & atone	Minister unto God
Sacrifices	Repeated	Once for all
Access	Restricted	Direct (through Christ)
Mediation	For people's sin	Christ is sole Mediator
Warfare	Bloodshed & intercession	Stand in truth & preach
Repentance	National/generational	Personal/relational

- It's used as a formula to "break territorial strongholds",
- It implies that believers must atone for sins already covered by the blood of Christ,
- Or it becomes a substitute for the true Gospel of grace and personal repentance.

Why it's problematic biblically:
- Nowhere in the New Testament are believers instructed to repent for the sins of their ancestors, cities, or nations to gain spiritual victory.
- Jesus already bore the full weight of sin, ours and the world's (John 1:29).
- Victory over the enemy comes through faith in the finished work of Christ, not through emotional or symbolic rituals (Colossians 2:13–15).
- Paul never practiced or taught this in his church-planting efforts in deeply pagan cities like Corinth, Ephesus, or Rome.

Identificational repentance might seem humble or sincere, but when used as a spiritual tactic to "unlock blessings" or "dismantle demonic structures," it distracts from the sufficiency of Christ and places the Church under legalistic striving rather than Gospel rest.

While the Old Testament does record examples of leaders repenting on behalf of others, those were specific to Israel's covenant and not a model for binding territorial spirits. In the New Covenant, we are called to preach the Gospel, renew minds, and walk in the authority already given, not to relive or repent for the sins of ancestors.

Wagner asserts that these methods were largely unknown to most Christians before the 1990s, marking a significant shift in spiritual warfare practices.

We Wrestle not...

Biblical Response:

Paul never instructed the Church to engage in "strategic warfare" over cities. Jesus didn't train His disciples to war against demonic hierarchies in the air. Instead, the early Church advanced by preaching the Gospel, healing the sick, making disciples, and confronting false doctrine, not by mapping out spirits over Rome, Corinth, or Ephesus.

When Paul described our warfare in 2 Corinthians 10:3–5, it was not about rebuking regional spirits but about pulling down strongholds in the mind, patterns of thinking that exalt themselves above the knowledge of Christ.

Jesus didn't teach His disciples how to pray against principalities; He taught them to pray, "Thy Kingdom come." He didn't give them strategies for cosmic warfare; He gave them authority to heal, teach, and demonstrate the Kingdom.

Territorial spirits

C. Peter Wagner's book ***Engaging the Enemy: How to Fight and Defeat Territorial Spirits***. In this book, Wagner promotes the idea of territorial spirits and the need for believers to strategically engage and defeat them through prayer.

Here's a paraphrased summary of his teaching, followed by a specific quote:

General Teaching Summary:

Wagner claims that high-ranking demonic powers (territorial spirits) are assigned by Satan to govern specific geographic regions, cities, or people groups. He advocates

We Wrestle not...

that Christians must "identify" these spirits through spiritual mapping, "engage" them through strategic intercession, and "defeat" them to open regions to the Gospel.

Specific Quote:

"Satan has assigned high-ranking members of his hierarchy of evil spirits to control nations, regions, cities, tribes, people groups, neighborhoods and other significant social networks of human beings throughout the world."
— **C. Peter Wagner, Engaging the Enemy, Regal Books, 1991**

This quote summarizes Wagner's central claim regarding territorial spirits.

Biblical Response:

There is no New Testament precedent for this teaching. The apostles never sought to engage territorial spirits. They entered cities, proclaimed Christ, and transformed hearts. The authority Jesus gave wasn't for wrestling spirits in the heavens, it was for casting out devils when they manifest on earth, healing the sick, and making disciples of all nations (Matthew 28:18–20).

In Acts, Paul did not "bind" a spirit over Athens. He reasoned with thinkers in the marketplace and preached the resurrected Christ. The warfare was not atmospheric, it was apostolic, strategic, and theological.

Prayer as warfare for leaders

Book: *'Prayer Shield'*

We Wrestle not...

Wagner emphasizes that leaders are "on the front lines" and need special intercessory protection because of the spiritual attacks they face in battle.

Biblical Response:

While interceding for leaders is biblical (Ephesians 6:19–20), the notion of a spiritual "front line" is foreign to the New Covenant. There is no elite class of spiritual soldiers. Every believer has been given armor. Every believer has been seated with Christ in heavenly places (Ephesians 2:6). And every believer is called to rest in the finished work of Christ.

The idea that leaders need a "shield of prayer" to survive demonic targeting subtly places more power in the hands of the devil than he has. It also fosters fear and hierarchy, not faith and unity. We are one body, protected not by vigilant intercession, but by abiding in Christ (John 15:4–5).

WARFARE AS DAILY PRACTICE

Books: *'The Beginner's Guide to Spiritual Warfare', 'Warfare Prayer', 'Praying with Power'*

These books encourage believers to engage in daily "warfare" prayers, binding spirits, pleading the blood, declaring authority, and pushing back darkness as part of their spiritual discipline.

Biblical Response:

The New Testament never commands us to bind the devil daily. Jesus said, "Abide in Me." Paul said, "Put on Christ." Our spiritual life is not a checklist of combat routines, it's a relationship rooted in righteousness, peace, and joy in the Holy Spirit (Romans 14:17).

We do not put on the armor of God like a suit every morning. We put on Christ once and for all (Galatians 3:27). Our armor is our identity. To live clothed in Christ is to be always protected, always empowered, always victorious.

THE GOSPEL OF REST, NOT RESTLESSNESS

What many believers call "warfare" is often spiritual anxiety wrapped in zeal. The greatest act of war a believer can engage in is to rest in Christ's victory and refuse to be moved by fear, lies, or false teaching.

"There remains a rest for the people of God... Let us therefore labor to enter that rest." — **Hebrews 4:9,11 (NKJV)**

The greatest warfare is the fight of faith, not the fight against demons. Paul told Timothy to *"fight the good fight of faith"* (1 Timothy 6:12), not the fight of spiritual combat. When believers spend their energy storming gates that Christ already kicked down, they unknowingly leave the place of peace and power.

CALLING THE CHURCH BACK TO KINGDOM CLARITY

Wagner's intentions may have been sincere, but sincerity cannot replace sound doctrine. His writings, though influential, have redirected many away from a Christ-centered, finished-work theology and into a spiritual frenzy of mapping, marching, and striving.

We Wrestle not…

This is not the way of the Kingdom.

Jesus didn't say the gates of hell would be stormed by prayer warriors. He said they would not prevail against the Church He is building (Matthew 16:18). Victory is not achieved through warfare, it is inherited through sonship.

The Church must return to rest, not reaction.

We Wrestle not…

Reflection & Discussion:

1. Have you ever found yourself striving in spiritual warfare rather than resting in Christ?
2. How does the concept of "putting on Christ" change your understanding of daily spiritual life?
3. What practices in your walk may be rooted more in fear than faith?
4. How would your spiritual habits change if you truly believed the enemy was already disarmed?
5. What does it look like for you to labor to enter rest instead of battle?

CHAPTER TEN
IDENTIFYING THE THIEF

"The thief does not come except to steal, and to kill, and to destroy. I have come that they may have life, and that they may have it more abundantly." — **John 10:10, NKJV**

Context Is King: Who Is the Thief?

John 10 is part of Jesus' extended discourse contrasting Himself, the Good Shepherd, with impostors. In verse 1, Jesus says, *"He who does not enter the sheepfold by the door, but climbs up some other way, the same is a thief and a robber."*

This sets the framework: the "thief" refers to those who bypass the legitimate means of access, those who do not come through Christ.

These include:
- False prophets
- False apostles
- Religious leaders
- Hirelings and uncalled ministers

Nowhere in this context is Satan or demonic spirits referenced directly. The "thief" is not contextually revealed as devil, but false leaders who harm the sheep.

The Pseudo Problem

In Matthew 7:15, Jesus warns, "Beware of false prophets [Greek: pseudoprophētēs], who come to you in sheep's clothing but inwardly they are ravenous wolves."
- Pseudo (Greek: pseudes) implies spurious, illegitimate, not authentic.
- A spurious prophet is not just wrong, they are unauthorized.
- The term carries the connotation of being fatherless, not born from or under legitimate spiritual authority.

This word echoes the concept of bastards (Greek: nothos, Hebrews 12:8), those not receiving correction or legitimate discipline. These individuals are unfathered, and therefore unformed in character and unfit for spiritual leadership.

The enemy called Fatherlessness

Paul declared, *"Though you have ten thousand instructors in Christ, yet you do not have many fathers"* **(1 Corinthians 4:15, NKJV).**

Apostolic order requires not just teachers, but fathers, those who give birth to, nurture, correct, and release sons in the faith.

False prophets often:
- Reject discipline
- Self-appoint
- Operate independently
- Exploit the sheep

We Wrestle not...

In this light, Jesus' warning about the thief is not satanic in nature but apostolic in tone. He was calling out a systemic leadership failure, men who went but were not sent.

What They Steal, Kill, and Destroy

Unauthorized leaders:
- Steal identity, truth, and Kingdom inheritance.
- Kill hope, potential, and faith through control and manipulation.
- Destroy lives by misrepresenting God and feeding on the sheep.

When Jesus said the thief comes to steal, kill, and destroy (John 10:10), He was not describing demonic activity, but the devastating effects of unauthorized spiritual leadership. False prophets, teachers, and apostles do not carry the Father's heart, and therefore, rather than feeding the sheep, they exploit and mislead them.

Let's break down how this unfolds:

They Steal the Kingdom

Jesus condemned the Pharisees for this very crime:

"Woe to you, scribes and Pharisees, hypocrites! For you shut up the kingdom of heaven against men; for you neither go in yourselves, nor do you allow those who are entering to go in." — **Matthew 23:13, (NKJV)**

Unauthorized leaders steal the Kingdom from the people when they:
- Preach another gospel that emphasizes law, fear, or self-effort instead of the message of the Kingdom.

- Replace Kingdom entrance (repentance and faith in Christ's lordship) with religious performance and denominational gatekeeping.

They Steal Identity

They Steal Identity by Robbing Sonship

At the heart of unauthorized teaching is a deliberate distortion of identity, not merely in general terms, but in withholding the revelation of sonship.

"A slave does not abide in the house forever, but a son abides forever." — **John 8:35, (NKJV)**

Rather than preaching the Gospel of the Kingdom that reveals sons, many leaders preach a gospel that:
- Elevates servanthood as identity, rather than a function.
- Keeps believers sin-conscious, rather than righteousness-aware.
- Teaches that God tolerates them rather than treasures them.

Key Contrasts Between False Identity and Sonship:

False Identity (Servant Mentality)	Kingdom (Sonship Mentality)
Defined by past sin	Defined by new birth
Motivated by fear and obligation	Motivated by love and inheritance
Always repenting, never resting	Resting in righteousness and growing in maturity

We Wrestle not...

Performing to be accepted	Accepted, therefore maturing in function
Trying to get in the House	Permanent heir in the Father's house
Needs constant affirmation	Carries confident authority

Unauthorized leaders steal identity when they:
- Call born-again sons "sinners saved by grace" rather than new creations born of God (2 Corinthians 5:17).
- Reduce the Gospel to behavior modification instead of identity transformation.
- Preach as though the cross made us better servants, instead of birthing us as sons.

This theft is subtle, but deadly. It:
- Keeps the Church in orphanhood rather than maturity.
- Produces spiritual dependence on leaders instead of confidence in the Father.
- Replaces intimacy with performance, and inheritance with striving.

They Steal Truth

Jesus said, *"I am the Way, the Truth, and the Life"* (John 14:6). Yet, many treat scripture (graphe) as truth itself, rather than letting it reveal the Logos, the Living Word who is Truth.
- Scripture is inspired, but it must point to Christ, or it becomes a weapon in the hands of religion.
- Unauthorized teachers use isolated verses to uphold tradition or personal doctrine, not to unveil the heart of the Father through the Son.

- In doing so, they steal the people's access to the unchangeable Truth, Jesus Himself, and replace it with filtered interpretations.

They Kill Hope, Potential, and Faith

"So then faith comes by hearing, and hearing by the word [rhema] of God." — **Romans 10:17, (NKJV)**

Faith does not come by clever ideas, moralism, or denominational traditions, it comes by hearing the revealed Word of God.

Unauthorized leaders kill hope and faith when they:
- Preach their own convictions instead of the King's commands.
- Share principles without presence.
- Offer motivational opinions rather than revelatory truth.

This suppresses the growth of God's people, limits their potential, and causes them to trust in man, not the Messiah.

They Destroy Through Parroted Theology

Many unauthorized leaders do not preach from revelation but regurgitation. They:
- Repeat what they've heard from others without testing it by the Spirit.
- Teach borrowed doctrines as if they were revealed truth.
- Speak without being sent and minister without having seen.

We Wrestle not...

As a result, they destroy lives, not by demonic force, but by misrepresenting God, misguiding the flock, and multiplying confusion in the Body.

Jesus, by contrast, gives life and brings the sheep into abundant, maturing, sonship-based living.

Jesus didn't warn of the devil or hi demons, he identifies thieves and robbers as those that come into the sheepfold with proper authorization.

Implications for the Warfare Narrative

If the thief is a person, not a principality, then the narrative of the thief must be understood relationally, not just mystically:
- Discernment is key.
- Spiritual battles are often fought with truth, correction, and apostolic order, not binding devils, but silencing deception.
- Apostolic ministry does not just war against the demonic, it restores sonship and calls out the thieves and robbers.

This exhaustive list of examples reveals the urgency for the Apostles to identify and disqualify the unauthorized leaders of their day.

Paul's Warnings

1. Hymenaeus and Alexander

"...holding faith and a good conscience. By rejecting this, some have made shipwreck of their faith, among whom are Hymenaeus and Alexander, whom I handed over to Satan

that they may learn not to blaspheme." — **1 Timothy 1:19–20, (ESV)**

2. Hymenaeus and Philetus
"Their talk will spread like gangrene. Among them are Hymenaeus and Philetus, who have swerved from the truth, saying that the resurrection has already happened. They are upsetting the faith of some." — **2 Timothy 2:17–18, (ESV)**

3. Demas (by implication)
"For Demas, in love with this present world, has deserted me and gone to Thessalonica." — **2 Timothy 4:10, (ESV)**

4. False apostles
"For such men are false apostles, deceitful workmen, disguising themselves as apostles of Christ." — **2 Corinthians 11:13, (ESV)**

5. The Judaizers (Galatians)
"I wish those who unsettle you would emasculate themselves!" — **Galatians 5:12, (ESV)**

Paul harshly rebukes those preaching circumcision and law as requirements for salvation. His suggestion is that those force feeding an obsolete doctrine of circumcision would castrate themselves in the process.

6. Those who preach another gospel
"But even if we or an angel from heaven should preach to you a gospel contrary to the one we preached to you, let him be accursed." — **Galatians 1:8, (ESV)**

Peter's Warning

7. False teachers among the people

We Wrestle not...

"But false prophets also arose among the people, just as there will be false teachers among you, who will secretly bring in destructive heresies..." — **2 Peter 2:1, (ESV)**

Peter continues in that chapter describing their greed, deception, and judgment. (See 2 Peter 2:1–22.)

John's Warning

8. Antichrists and false spirits
"Beloved, do not believe every spirit, but test the spirits to see whether they are from God, for many false prophets have gone out into the world." — **1 John 4:1, (ESV)**

9. Diotrephes
"...Diotrephes, who likes to put himself first, does not acknowledge our authority." — **3 John 1:9, (ESV)**

John calls him out for rejecting apostolic order and exalting himself in the Church.

Jude's Description

10. Ungodly intruders
"For certain people have crept in unnoticed who long ago were designated for this condemnation, ungodly people..."
— **Jude 1:4, (ESV)**

Jude goes on to describe them as shepherds feeding themselves, waterless clouds, and twice-dead trees.

In John 10:8 (NKJV), Jesus explicitly states:

"All who ever came before Me are thieves and robbers, but the sheep did not hear them."

We Wrestle not...

This verse is not referring to demons or Satan but to unauthorized human leaders, false messiahs, corrupt priests, Pharisees, and religious figures who assumed positions of authority without being sent by God. Jesus was confronting a religious system full of:
- Power-hungry rulers
- Legalistic gatekeepers
- Self-appointed "shepherds" who devoured the sheep instead of feeding them

The Shield of Sensitivity: How the Enemy Protects False Teachers

In today's Church culture, the enemy has done something cunning, not by hiding unauthorized teachers, but by making it socially awkward and politically incorrect to expose them.
- Truth is now labeled unloving
- Correction is considered harsh
- Doctrinal confrontation is called divisive

This shift has redefined spiritual discernment as "judgmentalism" and apostolic accountability as "church hurt."

The result?

Men's emotional responses are now prioritized over God's eternal standards.

The Culture of Nice vs. the Commission to Guard

Paul told Timothy:

We Wrestle not...

"Preach the word... rebuke, exhort, with all long suffering and doctrine. For the time will come when they will not endure sound doctrine..." — **2 Timothy 4:2–3, (NKJV)**

But we now live in a time when:
- Bold preaching is replaced with broad appeasement
- Rebuke is softened for fear of backlash
- Doctrinal soundness is optional if the preacher is popular

This isn't mercy, it's compromise masquerading as compassion.

Why This Matters

The New Testament Church was not afraid to name names, mark divisions, and silence false voices, for the protection of the flock. Today's Church, however, often:
- Platforms charisma over character
- Defends wolves because of their influence
- Sacrifices truth to maintain unity

But unity without truth is not biblical unity, it's bondage.

The strategy of the enemy is to silence spiritual fathers under the accusation of "being critical" while his own sons preach unchallenged lies.

So how can we graciously deal with the unauthorized teachers without arrogant judgment, but spiritual watchfulness?

Discernment Without Defamation

We must learn to judge righteously without slandering personally.

We Wrestle not…

"Do not judge according to appearance, but judge with righteous judgment." — **John 7:24, (NKJV)**

- We discern doctrine and fruit, not motives or eternal fate.
- We can warn the Church without attacking the individual.
- Paul named names to protect the Church, not to destroy reputations (e.g., Hymenaeus and Alexander).

Gracious watchfulness says: "This teaching leads to error" instead of "This person is evil."

Guard the Gate, Don't Patrol the Fence

Our primary assignment is not to go on witch hunts, but to guard the gate of influence where we've been set.

"Take heed to yourselves and to all the flock, among which the Holy Spirit has made you overseers…" — **Acts 20:28, (NKJV)**

Apostolic authority is local before it is global

- Gracious leaders do not assume oversight they haven't been given but steward the flock in their care with diligence.
- This means refusing to platform false teachers, and teaching truth clearly in contrast to error.

We Wrestle not...

Speak the Truth in Love

"...but, speaking the truth in love, may grow up in all things into Him who is the head, Christ..." — **Ephesians 4:15, (NKJV)**

- Truth without love becomes prideful.
- Love without truth becomes powerless.
- Truth spoken in love confronts, corrects, and cultivates growth.

A Kingdom leader can say:
- "This teaching is not consistent with Christ."
- "This doctrine is not producing mature sons."
- "This person's message bypasses the gate; Christ."

And do so with tears, not taunts.

Restore Those Who Will Receive

"Brothers, if someone is overtaken in any trespass, you who are spiritual restore such a one in a spirit of gentleness..." — **Galatians 6:1, (NKJV)**

- False teaching doesn't equal false teachers.
- Some just haven't grown to revelation that restructures their doctrine.
- Restoration is the goal, but it requires both repentance and re-submission to truth.

We Wrestle not…

Stay Fathered to Stay Faithful

Unauthorized men are often unfathered, so the best guard against becoming one is remaining submitted ourselves.
- Apostolic leaders stay correctable.
- We remain accountable.
- We model what we teach.

The grace to correct others flows from the humility of being corrected ourselves.

When the result of unauthorized leaders is as detrimental as it is, then it is understandable why it could appear the devil did it.

The Devil Didn't Do It, Disorder Did

In a world of spiritual blame-shifting, it's common to point to the devil when the Church suffers confusion, division, or collapse. But much of what we attribute to demonic warfare is actually the result of unauthorized, unsubmitted leadership.

"The heaven, even the heavens, are the Lord's; but the earth He has given to the children of men." — **Psalm 115:16, (NKJV**

God gave dominion to man, and in Christ, that dominion was restored, not to rule over each other, but to rule through righteousness, peace, and order.

We Wrestle not…

Chaos Is Not Demonic by Default

The enemy doesn't have the authority to create chaos in the Church, he relies on disorder among men to do that for him.
- When leaders go without being sent
- When doctrine is taught without revelation
- When charisma is platformed without character
- When fathering is abandoned for fame

…the devil doesn't have to attack, he simply waits.

A Smiling Enemy in the Shadows

When we blame him for what bad leadership has done:
- He hides in the shadows of our ignorance.
- He smiles over a strategic victory he didn't even have to fight for.
- He watches as the Church devours itself through disorder and disobedience.

Hell rejoices when the Church blames Satan for what sons refused to steward.

Responsibility Is Our Warfare

Real warfare is not shouting at devils, it's taking responsibility for the ground we've been given.
- The ground of truth
- The ground of government
- The ground of sound doctrine
- The ground of godly leadership

The moment we stop blaming demons and start confronting disorder, the devil loses his foothold.

These leaders tried to climb up some other way (John 10:1), bypassing God's order, authority, and gate, which is Christ Himself. That's why He declares Himself the Door (v. 7, 9) and the Good Shepherd (v. 11).

So in summary:
- The thief in John 10 is not the devil.
- It is leaders that "climbed up another way", particularly those who came before Christ and sought to control God's people without being authorized by the Father.

From Genealogy to Generation: The Shift in Priesthood Authority

Those who were before Him were appointed by genealogy, not the gate.

Under the Old Covenant, leadership, especially priesthood, was based on lineage. Only descendants of Aaron could serve as priests, and Levitical genealogy determined ministerial legitimacy (see Exodus 28:1; Numbers 3:10).

But in Christ, that genealogical system was fulfilled and replaced. Now, leadership is no longer conferred by bloodline or ancestry but by new birth and divine appointment.

"But as many as received Him, to them He gave the right to become children of God, to those who believe in His name: who were born, not of blood, nor of the will of the flesh, nor of the will of man, but of God." — **John 1:12–13, (NKJV)**

The New Covenant introduces a royal priesthood (1 Peter 2:9), one not based on tribe or family tree, but on spiritual regeneration and Christ's own priesthood (Hebrews 7:11–

We Wrestle not...

17). Jesus Himself was not from the tribe of Levi but from Judah, *"of which tribe Moses spoke nothing concerning priesthood"* (Hebrews 7:14).

The implications are significant:
- Christ, not ancestry, is the qualifier.
- Calling replaces pedigree.
- Sonship, not schooling, marks authority.
- Discipleship and spiritual fathering, not religious hierarchy, affirm and send leaders.

So when false leaders arise, those who *"climb up another way"*, they are often operating under Old Covenant mindsets or self-promotion, not Kingdom sonship.

This is why pseudoprophetes are so dangerous, they may have charisma or religious heritage, but they lack the commissioning of Christ and the correction of fathers.

Wolves in Wool: The Conscious Deception of Pseudo-Ministers

When Jesus warned, *"Beware of false prophets, who come to you in sheep's clothing, but inwardly they are ravenous wolves"* **(Matthew 7:15, NKJV)**, He was not describing people who were merely

Misguided, but those who were deliberately deceptive.
- "Sheep's clothing" is not an accident, it's a disguise.
- The wolf chooses to wear it.
- The false prophet is conscious of their falseness, they know they weren't sent, but they use religious garments, language, and authority to gain access to the flock.

This connects directly to the word "pseudo", a spurious person, not by mistake, but by intentional misrepresentation.

Workers of Iniquity: Operating Without Delegation

In Matthew 7:21–23, Jesus intensifies this rebuke:

"Many will say to Me in that day, 'Lord, Lord, have we not prophesied in Your name...? And then I will declare to them, 'I never knew you; depart from Me, you who practice lawlessness [iniquity]!'"

- The Greek word for lawlessness is anomia, meaning "without law" or illegal.
- These individuals were performing ministry acts, but without legal Kingdom authorization.
- The phrase *"I never knew you"* isn't a denial of relational awareness, it's a statement of unauthorized commission: *"I never knew you in the capacity in which you acted. I did not appoint you."*

This shows us:
- False prophets are not simply incorrect, they are illegitimate.
- They operated under their own will, not God's government.
- They went out unfathered, unformed, and unsent, yet cloaked themselves in spiritual garb to access God's people.

This also reinforces the need for apostolic order and spiritual fathering. In a Kingdom framework:
- Sonship is the prerequisite for sending.
- Delegation is never assumed, it is given.

We Wrestle not...

Sent by the Spirit, Sent by the House: Kingdom Order in Apostolic Sending

In Acts 13:1-3, we see a profound moment in early Church structure and Kingdom government:

"Now in the church that was at Antioch there were certain prophets and teachers... As they ministered to the Lord and fasted, the Holy Spirit said, 'Now separate to Me Barnabas and Saul for the work to which I have called them.' Then, having fasted and prayed, and laid hands on them, they sent them away." — **Acts 13:1-3, (NKJV)**

Then, in Acts 13:4, Luke adds this:

"So, being sent out by the Holy Spirit..."

Here's the revelation:
- The prophets and teachers at Antioch laid hands and sent them, a physical, communal, ecclesiastical act.
- But Luke says they were sent by the Holy Spirit.
- This isn't contradictory, it's complementary.

Apostolic sending through the local church is the mechanism by which the Spirit sends.

This reveals a Kingdom truth:
- The Holy Spirit works through order.
- Spiritual sending is not mystical isolation, it's communal recognition.
- Those who are truly called will be found ministering to the Lord, not self-promoting or platform-hunting.

This challenges the modern trend of:
- Self-appointed apostles
- Internet-ordained prophets

- Independent ministries with no accountability or fathering

Pseudo and the Thief

When Jesus says, *"He who does not enter the sheepfold by the door... is a thief and a robber"* (John 10:1), He's describing those who refuse the process of sending. They bypass the gate (Christ), the house (local church), and the order (apostolic government). These are the pseudo-ministers.

They may sound spiritual, but they:
- Were not set apart by prophetic confirmation
- Were not sent through corporate laying on of hands
- Were not recognized by the Body
- And therefore were not sent by the Holy Spirit

Apostolic sending is not just ceremonial—it is the Kingdom's divine commissioning protocol. And to bypass it is to declare oneself a thief, operating outside the gate.

Misdiagnosed Warfare: When Unauthorized Men Blame the Devil

By identifying the thief in John 10 not as Satan but as unauthorized leaders, we unveil a larger deception: much of what has been called "spiritual warfare" is not warfare at all, but the natural consequence of spiritual disorder.

In many circles, when ministries collapse, churches divide, or sheep are scattered, the phrase often follows:

"The devil is busy."

We Wrestle not...

But Scripture and context suggest otherwise:
- The scattering comes from hirelings, not hell (John 10:12–13).
- Destruction often follows false doctrine, not demonic attacks (2 Peter 2:1).
- Doctrines of devils do not emerge from demons teaching people, but from people teaching demonically-inspired lies (1 Timothy 4:1–2).

This points to a deeper issue:

Many unauthorized men, self-appointed, unfathered, and unformed, teach doctrines that open doors to confusion, and then blame the devil for the mess they caused.

Jesus reserved His harshest language not for demons, but for:
- Religious leaders (Matthew 23)
- False prophets (Matthew 7:15)
- Blind guides (Matthew 15:14)
- Lawless workers (Matthew 7:23)

These weren't demon-possessed individuals. They were simply:
- Unsent
- Unfathered
- Unauthoritative
- Unrepentant

A Kingdom Truth:

The devil doesn't have to destroy what we allow to collapse through disorder.

Just as Saul lost his kingship not by satanic warfare but by unauthorized sacrifice (1 Samuel 13), so many ministries fall

We Wrestle not…

not from demonic attack but from violation of order and misrepresentation of the King.

Conclusion

The Residue of the Unauthorized

What we often label as "spiritual warfare", or "the devil's attack" is in many cases simply the fallout from unauthorized leadership.

The residue of those who were not sent is mistakenly interpreted as the activity of Satan.

Church hurt.
Disappointment in leadership.
Wounds from fallen pastors.
Confusion from contradictory teachings.

These are not always demonic attacks, they are the inevitable consequence of men and women operating in calling without covering, ambition without appointment, passion without placement.

We've blamed the enemy for the messes that unfathered ministers and unsent voices have created. But if we spiritualize these consequences and ignore the root issue, the absence of divine order and apostolic sending, we will continue to see the Church stumble under the weight of self-appointed ministry.

This is not a demonic enterprise, it is a human disorder.

The Kingdom has an appointing structure.

We Wrestle not…

And where that order is rejected, the chaos is not spiritual warfare, it is the predictable harvest of misalignment.

Until we restore the pattern of sons being sent by fathers, of leaders laying hands on with fasting and confirmation, and of voices being tested before being trusted, we will keep calling manmade chaos a spiritual storm.

We Wrestle not…

Reflection Prompts

1. What does the context of John 10 reveal about the true identity of the thief?
2. How does the word "pseudoprophetes" expand your understanding of false leadership?
3. In what ways can spiritual leaders become thieves without even realizing it?
4. How does submitting to true spiritual fathering protect you from deception?
5. Why is it important to distinguish between demonic warfare and apostolic correction?

CHAPTER ELEVEN
AN OPEN INVITATION

The cross didn't just save individuals from sin; it recalibrated the spiritual legal system by which the enemy operated. Before the cross, humanity was under bondage to sin and death (Rom. 5:12–14), and Satan had broader access because of Adam's transgression. But after the cross, the default legal ownership of humanity shifted.

Humanity Was Bought and Paid For at the Cross

"You were bought at a price; do not become slaves of men."
— **1 Corinthians 7:23**

"...not with silver or gold... but with the precious blood of Christ..." — **1 Peter 1:18–19**

This means the ownership of mankind changed at Calvary. While not all are saved in experience (because of unbelief), all were ransomed. The blood didn't just forgive sin, it legally revoked the devil's unchallenged access to humanity.

The Devil Now Requires Willing Access

Before the cross, Satan operated with relative impunity, particularly under the Old Covenant, where sin gave him legal standing.

"The whole world lies under the sway of the wicked one."
— **1 John 5:19**

But after the cross, he was disarmed:

"Having disarmed principalities and powers, He made a public spectacle of them, triumphing over them in it [the cross]." — **Colossians 2:15**

Now, the devil is stripped of legal weapons and must rely on permission and open doors. These doors are:
- Unforgiveness
- Bitterness
- Occult practices
- Willful sin
- Agreement with lies
- Rebellion and dishonor

In essence: No door, no entry.

The Human Heart Remains the Gateway

Jesus knocks (Rev. 3:20), but so does the serpent, he just doesn't wait like Jesus does. He manipulates, projects, and tempts, trying to get you to open the door voluntarily.

This is why Paul tells believers:

"Do not give place to the devil." — **Ephesians 4:27 (NKJV)**

You can only give what is yours, and after the cross, your life is no longer under Satan's domain. He has no automatic right to you. He needs an invitation.

We Wrestle not...

Fewer Possessions, More Oppressions

After the cross, true demonic possessions seem far less prevalent, especially among believers. Why?
- Because now he needs a door.
- Because now Jesus legally owns the title deed to humanity.
- Because now the Spirit of God indwells those who believe, and Satan cannot dwell where God reigns.

What you see more frequently post-cross is:
- Oppression (external pressure)
- Influence (mental deception)
- Torment (through open doors)

But indwelling control? It now requires far more consent and corruption than before.

The Cross Closed the Default Door

Before:
- All were in Adam, and the devil had broad access through sin.

After:
- All were bought by Christ, and the devil lost the deed.
- The cross closed the universal door to Satan's dominion, but each person still holds the key to their own heart.

"Do you not know that to whom you present yourselves slaves to obey, you are that one's slaves..." — **Romans 6:16**

The blood of Jesus radically changed the devil's access to humanity. Now:
- He must tempt to gain access.
- He must deceive to gain consent.
- He must wait for an invitation, because the door belongs to you.

In the Kingdom, authority is always tied to willful agreement. God doesn't override human will, and neither does the enemy. The serpent seeks agreement, whether through deception, desire, or desperation. Satan doesn't kick in doors; he looks for cracks, legal footholds, through which to operate. Paul's instruction in Ephesians 4:27 wasn't a warning to unbelievers; it was an admonition to the Church: *"Give no place to the devil."*

The word *'place'* in Greek is topos, meaning region, seat of influence, opportunity, or jurisdiction. This suggests that the believer can yield territory that was never meant to be surrendered. When we open ourselves, through behavior, belief, or spiritual compromise, we permit a thief into the house.

THE DOOR OF THE HEART

"Behold, I stand at the door and knock. If anyone hears My voice and opens the door, I will come in to him and dine with him, and he with Me." — **Revelation 3:20, NKJV**

What a stunning picture. Though Jesus is Lord of all creation, though He formed us and knows our hearts, He still knocks. He doesn't force the door open. He doesn't invade. He invites. The heart is sacred territory to God, and even the Creator waits for permission to enter.

We Wrestle not...

The heart is a door to the soul, a spiritual gate that governs what we allow to influence, inhabit, or shape us. What we open our heart to gains access. Jesus approaches the heart with love, knocking gently. But the enemy is not so kind.

The devil cannot just enter a person's life. He has no key. So, he resorts to pressure, manipulation, deception, or desperation, trying to trick us into opening the door ourselves. Sometimes, it's through pain. Other times, through curiosity, trauma, or a longing for connection. Regardless of the method, the principle remains:

The only way in is if we open the door.

We are not defenseless. We are not unguarded. We are sealed by the Holy Spirit (Ephesians 1:13), and our lives are hidden with Christ in God (Colossians 3:3). But just as Jesus waits for our invitation, the enemy looks for our permission, given knowingly or unknowingly, to enter and influence.

A TRUE TESTIMONY: WHEN A DOOR WAS OPENED

When I was in high school, I led a Bible study and prayer group during lunch. One afternoon, a girl asked for prayer. She said it was a private matter and insisted that we speak alone. I agreed and stepped with her into a smaller adjacent room.

As I sat across from her, something unexpected happened. She began to speak, but the voice was not her own. It was unnaturally deep, distorted, and dark. I discerned immediately that a demonic presence had manifested. Not knowing what to do alone, I ran to get a friend to help me pray.

We Wrestle not...

We returned together and sat with her again. But as we began to pray, she turned her head toward my friend, and her face visibly morphed into something grotesque and inhuman. He was so terrified; he ran out of the room. I was left alone.

I stood to my feet. She stood too, and then something even more startling happened: she rose straight up off the ground. Hovering.

Having never encountered anything like this before, I leaned on the only authority I knew: "Come out in the name of Jesus!" I declared.

The voice inside her responded:
"I will come out of her, and into you."

Without wavering, I called on the name of Jesus again. In that instant, it was as if an unseen force grabbed her by the waist and hurled her across the room. She slammed into the wall and collapsed to the floor.

She was later delivered at our church. She told me she had been involved in occult practices, summoning spirits and commanding them. But she said something chilling: *"I thought they were serving me... but I was actually serving them."*

She had *"given place to the devil."*

A SECOND ENCOUNTER: THE SLITHERING SERPENT

Years later, while ministering at a small church in Florida, our team witnessed another startling encounter. After praise and worship, I was given the pulpit to preach. As I began,

We Wrestle not...

the rear doors of the sanctuary opened and a slender, middle-aged woman entered the room.

Without a word, she collapsed to the floor.

After lying there momentarily, she suddenly rose up in a cobra-like stance, her body arched and rigid, then began slithering down the center aisle like a serpent, moving unnaturally toward the front of the church.

Though the scene was intense, it was short-lived. As I stepped forward, I spoke the name and authority of Jesus over her, and instantly, she was set free. No dramatics. No extended confrontation. The power of His name broke the hold.

Later, it was confirmed that she had a history of involvement with both drugs and occult activity. She had opened her life to darkness through agreement with deception and substances.

The devil had an open invitation!

A DEMON IN THE CLOSET: THE HOUSE CALL

One quiet afternoon, I received an unusual phone call. A woman asked,
"Do you perform exorcisms on houses?"

I chuckled and replied, *"Well, I'm not sure I'd call it that, but how can I help?"*

She invited me to her home the next day. When I arrived, she nervously described disturbing experiences taking place in her house. I offered to pray through each room, and she agreed.

We Wrestle not...

Everything seemed normal, until I approached a closed bedroom door. I asked for permission to enter, and she consented. As soon as I stepped in, the atmosphere shifted.

Suddenly, I saw what appeared to be a miniature, gargoyle-like creature emerge from the closet. It darted into a corner, then across the room, and finally perched on the windowsill. It looked terrified. I said,
You can't stay here. Leave."

It jumped out the window and vanished.

I stepped back into the hallway and called the woman into the room. I told her plainly, *"There's something in this closet that gave that spirit a right to be here."*

She searched through the shelves and found a Ouija board. Her young adult son had recently moved back home and had been using the board in that very room. That object had become a legal point of access, an instrument of invitation.

The devil had an open invitation!

A DIFFERENT DOOR: UNFORGIVENESS

Not every demonic influence comes through rituals or objects. Some doors are less obvious, but just as spiritually dangerous. One such door is unforgiveness.

The words of Jesus are sobering:

"And his master was angry, and delivered him to the torturers until he should pay all that was due to him. So My heavenly Father also will do to you if each of you, from his heart, does not forgive his brother his trespasses." —
Matthew 18:34–35, NKJV

We Wrestle not...

Forgiveness is not a mere emotional choice, it is a spiritual principle of access. When we withhold forgiveness, we hand the enemy grounds to torment and oppress. Jesus warned that bitterness could result in being delivered to tormentors, not because God is cruel, but because spiritual laws are real. Unforgiveness opens a door to torment.

A VISION OF INFIRMITY

During my Bible school years, I was visiting my aunt's home when I walked into the kitchen and met her neighbor for the first time. As I greeted her, something unusual happened. I suddenly saw a bat-like creature wrapped around her back, its claws gripped tightly around her chest, digging into her heart.

I had never seen this woman before, nor had I ever seen anything like that in my life. But I immediately knew this was infirmity. I asked if she was sick, and she confirmed it, she had just been diagnosed with leukemia.

I began to pray for her. As I did, I heard the Lord speak to my heart:
"She must forgive."

I gently asked her if there was someone she needed to forgive. She nodded and said she believed she knew exactly who it was. Right there at the kitchen table, she released that person in forgiveness.

At the very moment she spoke words of release, I saw that bat-like spirit lose its grip and fly away.

That day, I was reminded that sometimes it's not a Ouija board or ritual that opens the door, but a wound unhealed and a grudge unresolved. Bitterness, like the occult, gives place to the devil.

THE ROTTENNESS OF BONES

Years ago, I was invited to minister at a church in Michigan. As I prepared for the evening, I sensed the Lord speak something unusual to my spirit:

"I'm going to heal some people tonight, but you will not pray for healing."

When I arrived at the church and was called forward to speak, I again heard the Lord say:

"Now call forward anyone with osteoporosis, arthritis, or bone disease."

Eleven people came to the altar. I stood before them, ready to pray, when the Lord whispered again:

"Do not pray for healing."

Then came the instruction:
"Tell them to forgive those they are bitter toward."

At first, I questioned it. I thought, *"Lord, I didn't call them up here to confess bitterness, I called them up to be healed."*

But then, I understood: the infirmity was not the root, bitterness was. Scripture declares:

"A sound heart is life to the body, but envy (bitterness) is rottenness to the bones." — **Proverbs 14:30, (NKJV)**

We Wrestle not...

Bitterness is not just an emotional issue, it can manifest physically, especially in the bones. One by one, those standing at the altar began to forgive. As they released others, they themselves were released, not just from bitterness, but from the affliction that had settled in their bodies.

They didn't need healing prayer, they needed to close a door.

The Apostle John prayed:

"Beloved, I pray that you may prosper in all things and be in health, just as your soul prospers." — **3 John 2, (NKJV)**

Their physical health was directly tied to the condition of their souls. That night, they received healing, not just in their bones, but in their hearts. What medicine or intercession could not resolve, forgiveness did. They had given place to the devil through bitterness, but Jesus came to shut the door and set them free.

CHAPTER TWELVE
BINDING AND LOOSING

Binding and loosing is apostolic, not emotional.

This authority was never meant to be driven by spiritual hype or emotional intensity. It is not something activated by volume or desperation. Binding and loosing are judicial decisions, not spur-of-the-moment reactions. Apostles were entrusted with stewardship over doctrine, Church order, and the application of heavenly will on earth. They didn't treat it as a mystical phrase; they treated it as legal representation of Heaven's government.

True apostolic binding involves forbidding things that violate the spirit of the Kingdom (e.g., false doctrine, sinful practices, corrupt leadership). Loosing involves releasing or permitting things in alignment with Christ's nature (e.g., reconciliation, liberty, truth, forgiveness). This isn't mystical, it's judicial.

When the Church is functioning apostolically, binding and loosing becomes a deliberate, discerning act based on Kingdom alignment, not emotional reactions or sensationalized prayers.

It's about judgment and stewardship, not yelling at spirits of allergies or traffic delays.

We have spiritualized everything so much that common inconveniences are now seen as demonic interference. Traffic jams are blamed on territorial spirits. Sickness is rebuked as if every cough has a devil behind it. This kind of thinking distracts from the true purpose of spiritual authority.

God didn't give us keys to bind flat tires or rebuke minor inconveniences. He gave us Kingdom keys to unlock spiritual understanding, govern righteous behavior, and protect the integrity of the Church.

This misuse is often birthed out of sincere zeal but misplaced theology. If everything is the devil, then nothing is. And if binding and loosing is applied to trivial matters, it loses its weight for serious issues.

Jesus was not instructing us to loose angels over our finances or bind demons from coffee shops.

Jesus never demonstrated, taught, or endorsed the idea that believers should send angels to do errands or patrol parking lots. This kind of "spiritual micromanagement" treats Kingdom authority like a magical spellbook rather than a divine commission.

Scripture teaches that angels respond to the word of the Lord (Psalm 103:20), not our verbal commands. We don't direct angelic traffic; we partner with the Kingdom's will.

Likewise, nowhere in the New Testament do apostles "bind" spirits over cities, marketplaces, or everyday nuisances. Instead, they focused on proclaiming truth, building the Church, correcting false doctrine, and demonstrating Christ's reign. That's the pattern.

We Wrestle not...

Binding and loosing are for doctrinal decisions, Church discipline, and Kingdom agreement.

This is where the true weight of this teaching lands. The Church has been given the responsibility to discern what aligns with the King and what does not. That includes teachings, behavior, leadership, relationships, and more.

In Matthew 18:15–20, Jesus used binding and loosing in the context of church correction and reconciliation. The point was not about devils, but about how we steward relationships and truth within the Body.

The Early Church Used This Authority to Govern, Not Battle

The early Church didn't interpret Jesus' teaching on binding and loosing as permission to "war in the spirit." Instead, they governed through apostolic agreement, teaching, and correction.

In Acts 15, the apostles loosed Gentiles from circumcision requirements through prayerful consensus. In 1 Corinthians 5, Paul bound an unrepentant man by excluding him from the church. In 2 Corinthians 2, he loosed the same man through restoration and forgiveness.

These actions reflect the judicial and Kingdom nature of Jesus' words.

The Keys of the Kingdom: Access, Not Incantation

Jesus made this declaration after Peter's confession of His Messiahship. This moment marked a transfer of Kingdom access from the old religious system to the ekklesia, His called-out governing body.

Keys Represent Authority, Not Magic

In Scripture, keys symbolize authority, stewardship, and delegated access. The one who holds the keys controls entry, governs access, and unlocks restricted realms.

- Isaiah 22:22 speaks of the "key of the house of David" being laid upon Eliakim's shoulder, a clear symbol of governmental authority.
- Revelation 3:7 shows Jesus holding the key of David, opening doors no one can shut.

Jesus did not say, "I give you the keys to the Kingdom," which would imply entrance. He said, "I give you the keys of the Kingdom", indicating the Church already belongs inside the Kingdom and is now entrusted with operating its doors and decrees.

Keys Unlock, Enforce, and Administrate

The keys are not weapons to wave in the air; they are legal instruments to:

- Unlock revelation (see Luke 11:52, where Jesus rebukes religious leaders for taking away the key of knowledge),
- Authorize access to Kingdom truth and membership (Acts 2:38–41),
- Shut out falsehood and protect Kingdom integrity (Galatians 1:8–9).

We Wrestle not…

When Peter used the keys in Acts 2, he opened the door to Jews.

In Acts 10, the door was opened to Gentiles through Cornelius.

These were not mystical experiences, they were apostolic proclamations of what Heaven had already authorized.

The Church Holds Keys to Govern, Not Bind Spirits

Far from commanding angels or locking down spirits, the keys are meant to:

- Govern doctrine (Titus 1:9–11),
- Establish leadership (1 Timothy 3),
- Permit or restrict behaviors in alignment with the King's heart.

We are not instructed to "use our keys" to silence territorial spirits or unlock parking spaces. Rather, we are entrusted with Kingdom wisdom, discernment, and decision-making.

The Church becomes a gatekeeper, not a gate stormer.

Kingdom Sons Don't Fight with Keys, They Build With Them

Imagine someone trying to fight with a key. It's absurd. Keys are made to unlock doors and authorize entry, not to swing at enemies.

Likewise, sons of the Kingdom are called to:

- Unlock identity in others,

We Wrestle not...

- Open understanding of Scripture,
- Shut down false doctrine,
- Unlock gifts, callings, and destiny.

The key is the Word of the Kingdom (Matthew 13:19). Every time you preach, teach, or decree the truth of Jesus and His reign, you're using the keys of the Kingdom.

Summary Insight: We Don't Use Keys to Fight the Devil, We Use Keys to Reveal the King

The Church does not bind the devil using keys, it opens the Kingdom to people.

We do not storm Heaven with warfare language, we represent Heaven through righteous governance, sound doctrine, and Spirit-led agreement.

Keys symbolize delegated authority and access. Jesus gave the Church keys 'of the Kingdom' (not 'to' it), indicating that we steward the Kingdom's rule. We use keys to unlock revelation, open access to salvation, and protect truth, not to control spirits. The early Church used these keys to open doors to Jews (Acts 2) and Gentiles (Acts 10), establish doctrine (Acts 15), and uphold righteousness.

Keys are not weapons, they are instruments of trust. Kingdom sons don't fight with keys, they build with them.

Redeeming the Vocabulary of Victory

Our language must shift from fear-based, warfare clichés to truth-based, Kingdom decrees. Instead of crying out like orphans, we speak as sons. Our mouths are not for spiritual flailing, they are for prophetic framing. We must stop

We Wrestle not...

parroting battle language and start declaring the King's finished work.

Language: Greek Words with Jewish Roots

- The Greek words "bind" (δέω, deo) and "loose" (λύω, luo) were commonly used in legal and judicial contexts. But more importantly, these were Hebraic expressions long used by Jewish rabbis and teachers.
- In rabbinic Hebrew, the equivalent terms (asar for bind, hitir for loose) referred to the authority to forbid or permit actions according to Torah interpretation. This was the legal power of the rabbis and Sanhedrin.
- The Jewish Mishnah and Talmud both preserve this usage. For example, the Mishnah says, *"The school of Shammai binds and the school of Hillel looses."* This doesn't mean they're wrestling demons, it means one school forbade something that the other permitted.

So, when Jesus said He would give His disciples authority to bind and loose, His Jewish audience clearly understood it as judicial authority, not exorcistic.

Culture: Rabbinic and Synagogue Authority

- In Jewish custom, binding and loosing was about interpretation and enforcement. The rabbis, and later synagogue leaders, had authority to:
- Interpret Torah (i.e., determine what was forbidden or permitted).
- Enforce communal discipline (e.g., excommunication).

- Restore individuals who repented.
- Jesus applied this rabbinic framework to His ecclesia (church) but redefined the authority. Instead of relying on tradition or Pharisaic interpretation, His followers would bind and loose according to Heaven's will, led by His Spirit and grounded in His teaching.
- In Matthew 18, Jesus is building on that cultural structure. The "two or three witnesses" and the process of escalating a private offense to a public matter follow Torah guidelines (see Deuteronomy 19:15). He was showing how the new Kingdom community should govern itself in righteousness.

Application: Apostolic Authority, Not Mystical Power

- This context explains why Paul and the apostles used similar methods of judgment:
- Paul "binds" the unrepentant man in 1 Corinthians 5, handing him over for correction.
- He "looses" him in 2 Corinthians 2, calling for his restoration.
- The Jerusalem Council in Acts 15 uses apostolic agreement to loose Gentiles from the law of circumcision.

All of this reflects Jesus' original cultural and linguistic framework, not mystical spiritual warfare but spiritual

We Wrestle not...

Reflection Prompts

1. What are some warfare phrases you've used in prayer or teaching that are rooted in tradition rather than Kingdom truth?
2. How has your language shaped your understanding of your role, as a son or a soldier?
3. Do you see binding and loosing as legal authority or spiritual combat? How does Scripture reshape that view?
4. How can you begin to shift your vocabulary to reflect your placement in Christ rather than fear of the enemy?
5. What keys has God entrusted to you, and how are you using them to open hearts, release truth, or govern with wisdom?
6. Write a short decree in your own words that reflects your Kingdom identity and authority.

CHAPTER THIRTEEN
Prophetic Strategies

Introduction: Redefining Warfare, Waging with the Prophecies

This chapter reclaims the biblical meaning of 'warfare' as taught in the New Covenant, especially as it relates to prophecy.

Many believers today hear the word 'warfare' and immediately imagine a cosmic battle between good and evil, where they are expected to fight the devil head-on, shouting at demons or engaging in spiritual combat. But Paul offers a different picture when he speaks to Timothy:

'This charge I commit to you, son Timothy, according to the prophecies previously made concerning you, that by them you may wage the good warfare.' **(1 Timothy 1:18, NKJV)**

This warfare is not a fight against devils in the sky, it is the internal, strategic work of holding fast to what God has spoken, especially when circumstances tempt us to doubt, delay, or give up.

Prophecies and promises are not weapons we swing wildly in spiritual battles; they are divinely given strategies that secure our identity, direct our purpose, and anchor us in endurance. To wage a good warfare by the prophecies means to align ourselves with God's declared plan and resist anything, in thought, emotion, or circumstance, that seeks to pull us away.

We Wrestle not...

In this chapter, we will break down how biblical warfare is about faithfulness, not combat; alignment, not struggle; and strategy, not striving. We will dismantle the false notion of cosmic dualism and show that the believer's true battle is the fight to believe, hold fast, and walk in what God has already accomplished.

Prophecies as Strategic Tools

'By which have been given to us exceedingly great and precious promises, that through these you may be partakers of the divine nature...' **(2 Peter 1:4, NKJV)**

Prophetic words and promises are Kingdom tools. They help us hold identity, purpose, and direction when circumstances contradict what God has said.

What Are We Actually Fighting?

Paul clarifies: *'Fight the good fight of faith...'* **(1 Timothy 6:12, NKJV)**. We are not fighting devils, we are fighting unbelief. **Hebrews 4:11 (NKJV)** says, *'Let us therefore be diligent to enter that rest, lest anyone fall according to the same example of disobedience.'* True warfare happens when we are tempted to doubt God's word, when circumstances seem opposite of the promise **(Romans 4:20–21)**, or when we face delay and discouragement **(Hebrews 6:12)**.

Prophetic Strategies in Action

Prophetic promises function as strategies to:
- **Establish Identity**: reminding us of who we are and whom we belong to.
- **Set Direction**: clarifying the journey and purpose.

We Wrestle not...

- **Fuel Endurance:** strengthening us when timelines stretch long.
- **Confront Contradiction**: anchoring us when reality seems at odds with heaven.

The True Battlefield: The Mind
'For the weapons of our warfare are not carnal but mighty in God for pulling down strongholds...' **(2 Corinthians 10:4–5, NKJV).**

These strongholds are not demons in the air, they are arguments, mindsets, and thoughts that resist Christ's truth. The Greek word 'strateía' means a military campaign or strategy, not random acts of combat. Our New Covenant battle is fought by renewing the mind **(Romans 12:2)**, holding thoughts captive **(2 Corinthians 10:5)**, and standing in Christ's finished work **(Colossians 2:15)**.

Practical Prophetic Strategies

- Rehearse prophetic words over your life daily.
- Declare God's truth aloud, especially in moments of contradiction.
- Keep a journal of promises fulfilled and in progress.
- Stay connected to a faith community for strength and accountability.

Breaking the Myth of Cosmic Dualism

We are not caught in a cosmic back-and-forth war between equal forces. Christ has already disarmed rulers and authorities **(Colossians 2:15, NKJV)**. Our task is not to expand the victory but to enforce it through faith and alignment.

We Wrestle not…

Final Charge

Prophetic strategies are not magic formulas or shouting matches. They are Kingdom-aligned tools that shape our thoughts, reinforce our faith, and guide us through contradiction.

Strategy is not the fight, it's the framework. God's strategy is Christ. His plan is rest, renewal, and reign. The fight is not to achieve the victory but to remain aligned with the strategy. Our warfare is to stay faithful to the Word, disciplined in thought, and unmoved by contradiction.

We Wrestle not...

Reflection Prompts

1. What prophetic promises or words are you currently standing on?
2. Where have you been tempted to doubt or waver?
3. How can you practically anchor yourself in God's strategy this week?
4. What mindsets need renewing considering God's promises?

FINAL CHAPTER
AUTHORIZED SONS

"Behold, I give you the authority to trample on serpents and scorpions, and over all the power of the enemy, and nothing shall by any means hurt you." — **Luke 10:19, NKJV**

The war is over.
The King has risen.
The enemy is disarmed.
And we, the sons of the Kingdom, have not been left to fight, we've been authorized to reign.

This final chapter is not a call to arms but a call to alignment. It is the consummation of all Christ accomplished and the summary of what He left us with: not power to war, but authority to rule.

Authority vs. Power: Understanding the Divine Distinction

There is a vital distinction between dunamis (power) and exousia (authority). The modern Church often confuses the two, pursuing raw spiritual power as though warfare depends on strength. But Jesus never told us to fight the devil, He told us to walk in authority.

- Power (dunamis) is the capacity to act.
- Authority (exousia) is the right to act.

Power may impress demons.
Authority commands them.

We Wrestle not...

Jesus said: *"I give you authority over all the power of the enemy..."* (Luke 10:19). He didn't promise more dunamis than Satan. He gave us jurisdiction over his force.

Like a police officer who doesn't need more strength than the criminal, we don't need more spiritual force, we need faith in the badge, the seal of heaven backing our assignment.

The Centurion's Revelation: Faith Rests in Authority

"Only speak a word, and my servant will be healed. For I also am a man under authority..." — **Matthew 8:8–9**

The Roman centurion wasn't a theologian, but he grasped something most religious leaders missed: Jesus didn't need to come in power. His word carried authority.

Jesus was astonished, saying: "I have not found such great faith in all of Israel." Why? Because real faith doesn't beg for force, it rests in rightful position.

The centurion didn't need Jesus to fight, he trusted Him to rule.

This is Kingdom faith: not "*God, please move!*" but "*God has already spoken.*"

The Cross Was Not a Battle, It Was a Blowout

"And having disarmed principalities and powers, He made a public spectacle of them, triumphing over them in it." — **Colossians 2:15**

We Wrestle not...

At the cross:
- The enemy was crushed (Genesis 3:15)
- Death was destroyed (Hebrews 2:14)
- His claims were canceled (Colossians 2:14)

Satan is not resisting God's rule. He is subject to it.

He still has dunamis (he can deceive, tempt, influence), but he has no authority. He is like a squatter in a house that no longer belongs to him, he only remains where no one enforces the deed.

Pentecost Was Not Power to Fight, But Power to Die

"You shall receive power (dunamis) when the Holy Spirit has come upon you; and you shall be witnesses [Greek: martus] ..." — **Acts 1:8**

Pentecost was not empowerment for battle, but empowerment for surrender.
- Martus means witness, unto death.
- The dunamis of Pentecost was not for warfare, but for martyrdom.
- The power given was not to wage war, but to bear witness, suffer well, and preach the Gospel with unwavering boldness.

If Christ intended us to fight devils, He would have given us militant might. Instead, He gave us Holy Ghost courage to lay down our lives in victory.

We Are More Than Conquerors

"Yet in all these things we are more than conquerors through Him who loved us." — **Romans 8:37**

We Wrestle not...

To conquer means to win.

To be more than a conqueror means you inherit the victory without even entering the fight.

Jesus conquered.
We enforce.

This is what authority does: it places you in rest, not in battle. We are not on the frontlines, we are seated in heavenly places in Christ (Ephesians 2:6).

The Instrument of Victory Is Authority

"And He put all things under His feet and gave Him to be head over all things to the Church..." — **Ephesians 1:22–23**

The Head has already won.
The Body now moves with delegated dominion.

When you know who you are and where you're seated, you stop striving and start standing.
- You don't scream at devils, you rest in your assignment.
- You don't chase darkness, you turn on the light.
- You don't rebuke every storm, you speak peace because you are in the boat with the King.

Rest Is the Weapon

"The God of peace will soon crush Satan under your feet."
— **Romans 16:20**

Not the God of war.

We Wrestle not…

Not the God of fire.
The God of peace.

Peace crushes serpents because it proves you are not moved.

Authority is not loud, it is immovable.

You don't have to fight when you know you reign.

This Is Our Inheritance

Christ left us with authority, not anxiety.
He commissioned us to stand, not strive.
He made us sons, not spiritual soldiers in fear of a defeated devil.

We are the sons of the Kingdom.
We are seated, sealed, and sent.
We rule not by might, but by delegation from the Throne.

So now we live not to fight, but to enforce.
We live not to panic, but to govern from peace.

The serpent is under our feet.
The throne is occupied.
The Son is risen.
And we are authorized.

We Wrestle not…

Reflection prompt:

1. How does understanding the difference between power and authority shift your spiritual posture?
2. Have you ever tried to "gain power" when Jesus had already given you authority?
3. In what ways can you begin walking in your authority instead of reacting in fear?
4. What does it mean to be "more than a conqueror" in your everyday walk?
5. How does rest itself become a weapon against the schemes of the enemy?

www.ingramcontent.com/pod-product-compliance
Lightning Source LLC
Chambersburg PA
CBHW050141170426
43197CB00011B/1922